WRITING QUALITY

A Guide

KEN AND ELAINE MOON

Wrightbooks

First published in 1996
Wrightbooks Pty Ltd
PO Box 270
Elsternwick
Victoria 3185

ACN 007 050 277

Ph: (03) 9532 7082
Fax: (03) 9532 7084

National Library of Australia
Cataloguing-in-publication data:

Moon, Kenneth, 1928-
  Writing Quality Fiction - A Guide
  Includes index.
  ISBN 1 875857 21 4.
  1. Fiction - Authorship. 2. Fiction - Technique.
  3. Creative writing. I. Moon, Elaine. II. Title.
808.3

Cover design by Rob Cowpe
Printed in Australia by Australian Print Group.

ISBN: 1 875857 21 4

Contents

1

Introduction

"And what are you reading, Miss ---?"

"Oh! it is only a novel!" replies the young lady; while she lays down her book with affected indifference, or momentary shame.

In short, *only* some work in which the greatest powers of the mind are displayed, in which the most thorough knowledge of human nature, the happiest delineation of its varieties, the liveliest effusions of wit and humour, are conveyed to the world in the best chosen language.

NORTHANGER ABBEY, Jane Austen

What this GUIDE sets out to do, is to uncover those skills and techniques that underlie the writing of successful fiction. It is for people who are *seriously* serious about their writing. One quick canter through this GUIDE though, will not, sadly, get you instantly published. Any book or course claiming such, is skinning you! Indeed, to get the insights these pages offer, you will need to read carefully and closely; and to re-read and probably re-re-read. Not just the text either; but also, and perhaps more so, the many examples offered or directed to. Learning about writing is hard work. Almost as hard, in fact, as the actual writing itself. That's why, up there at the top of the profession, there's so much room and so little real competition!

Understanding the craft of fiction — along with practice in the techniques, reasonable talent and that inner compulsion to write, that *will* to succeed — should give the apprentice writer every chance of creating works which will eventually appear in print. Our GUIDE also offers to writers already moderately

1

successful, some opportunity to extend and deepen their understanding of their craft.

Now to clear some ground.

First, what is fiction?

We can, for our purposes, ignore the fascinating but sometimes mind-numbing 'new theory' of the past several decades, and simply reply: fiction is 'a tale told', what the eighteenth century termed 'fable'. Hence, we can look not only at the most obvious forms of storytelling, like novel and short story, but also at drama like Shakespeare's ANTONY AND CLEOPATRA and Arthur Miller's THE CRUCIBLE — even, if we wished, at narrative verse like Henry Lawson's "The Ballad of the Drover".

Indeed, this sort of overlap of genre does occur within fiction itself, as in Virginia Woolf's THE WAVES. Though her work has no real plot, it is usually considered a novel. It is entirely a series of monologues, speeches, delivered by six characters turn and turn about, so it has the actual form of drama. Yet, the prose is so dense with imagery and cadence that it is itself really closest to poetry.

This GUIDE, then, is directed primarily towards those looking to write novels and short stories; but it will for discussion and example draw on whatever kinds of fiction seem likely to prove most helpful at any particular point. Also, because the best way to learn about writing is from other successful authors, there will be very few pages here that do not refer to, or quote directly from, such published authors. That is, both *how it's done;* and examples of *it being done.*

QUALITY FICTION

Thus far has been about writing fiction — fiction generally. Yet, our title specifies QUALITY fiction. So?

We use this term to refer to the most 'successfully realised' fiction published, through from High Culture to Pulp. Producing fiction is a craft shared by William Shakespeare and Charles Dickens and Stephen King and that whole stable of Mills and Boon writers who each turn out perhaps half a dozen romance titles per year.

Some of these authors deal with weighty matters, exploring and illuminating deep human experience; while others offer plots primarily cliff-hanging or Cinderella-reassurances, pretty much as brief escape from those weighty human experiences. Most of these authors write for income, though a few are free of any such constraints. Some write novels and/or short stories; some, plays; a few, narrative verse; and you might want to include movie and tele-drama scripts and fictionalised biography.

All these, however, deal at least to an extent with plot and theme. All employ narrative; all people this narrative with characters who, from time to time, engage in dialogue; all this occurring in a setting, with a structure.

All writers, then, can and should respect what other writers have achieved. All writers can likewise learn from others. That's why this book casts its net so widely. Let's go for the quality in writing craft, learn from the most professional on offer, wherever, without prejudice. When Baz Lurhmann went into Fox to sell ROMEO AND JULIET as a movie, an intermediary present quipped: 'You got a great story here guys. Just don't mention the Shakespeare thing!'

Perhaps another question provoked by 'quality' in the title is: what does this GUIDE offer, that is not already on city bookshop shelves, many times over?

Books about the nature of fiction are customarily written by academics at universities who, while they understand a great deal about the way fiction works, have for the most part not actually produced any. Books about writing fiction, on the other hand, come more often from practising writers, with a 'workshop' and indeed entrepreneurial approach. An advantage of this present volume is that we — its authors — for a time made a living from freelance writing; and have, too, taught Eng. Lit. at universities for many years. We are thus well placed to bring together the best of both approaches, the more theoretical and the more practical.

Knowing how to do it, is what will get those pages running off for you. *Understanding* what makes a fictional structure cohere and engage, is what comes to your rescue when instinct and intuition have dumped on you and you're trying to sort out what's packed up with structure or dialogue, or why your work stopped flowing and you can't see where to head.

SHOWING NOT TELLING

WRITING QUALITY FICTION, therefore, offers opportunity to learn from many of the most successful authors ever, following the dictum: 'Don't tell, show.' Whatever your chosen area — thrillers or mood tales, fantasy or slice-of-life, sci-fi or domestic character studies, romances or adventure, Westerns or true confession, for children or for young adults, the comic novel or the literary piece, three-act play or ballad, four pulps a year or the single ten-years-to-write-and-based-on-my-own-life tome — whatever, you will be doing your apprenticeship with the proven quality!

Those who aim for the stars, it has been remarked, shoot highest.

While the examples we take will be drawn from a wide range of authors, three works in particular will be concentrated upon for discussion. This will allow you to become closely familiar with those three, and enable us to explore components within each work in relation one to another. For example, much plot is generated by character. Now, it would be rather unproductive to exemplify characterisation from one novel, ignoring its generating of plot in that work; and then to draw on some other novel for an example of plot, without reference to its dependence on the characters there. If the one novel is used to exemplify both characterisation and plot, we can trace their linkages.

The three works that are referred to most frequently in this Guide are: Emily Bronte's WUTHERING HEIGHTS, R.D. Salinger's THE CATCHER IN THE RYE and Katherine Mansfield's short-story "Bliss". One English, one American, one Antipodean. One from the mid-nineteenth century, one from just before the Swinging Sixties and one from earlier this century. A tragic novel, a comic novel, and the title story from a collection of somewhat subversive short stories. Two women authors, and one man.

Why, these three particular works?

For one thing, as already emphasised, they're quality. Readers, either over generations or in large numbers within our own time, have voted with their bookshelves, library cards, Christmas presents ... or however readers do vote. So the chosen authors must be doing something successfully?

These titles have been selected, too, for the very practical reason that they are available in inexpensive paperback. Indeed, many of you will already have them; but if you don't, and you want to get the best out of WRITING QUALITY FICTION, get 'em! You really *do* want to write, remember?

Other works of fiction drawn on for illustration and discussion are listed in the Appendix. Australian and New Zealand titles predominate. It would be of advantage, though it certainly isn't essential, to read several of these too.

Now to something about each of those three main titles and the reasons for their selection.

ONE MID-NINETEENTH CENTURY MASTERPIECE

WUTHERING HEIGHTS was written in the 1840s by Emily Bronte, daughter of an Irish clergyman in a moorland town in Yorkshire, England. It is her only published novel; she died in her late twenties, having destroyed a second, incomplete manuscript. Her sister Charlotte wrote novels too, the best known being JANE EYRE; and so did another sister, Anne. Emily's brother Branwell was likewise talented, particularly with paint; but he seems to have been the quintessential self-destroyer and died finally of (probably) drug abuse. Emily, who had been particularly close to him, went into an immediate decline and died herself, of tuberculosis, within weeks of her brother's funeral.

There is a popular view of Emily as a solitary eccentric living in some romantic bubble out on the wild moors, dreaming Byronic dreams; but in reality her world also included all the books and contemporary journals of her father's library, a regular stream of young university men through the parsonage, the better part of a year at a state-of-the-art school in Belgium where her achievements in writing, music and languages were remembered years after; and Emily was the one who successfully managed the investments the family inherited from Aunt Branwell!

WUTHERING HEIGHTS was chosen because millions of readers, past and present, have judged it one of the greatest works of literature. It has been made into numerous movies and at least one play. The novel has a compelling plot. (How those nineteenth century writers could tell a story!) It has also strong characterisation, powerful background, an interesting structure and a most intriguing method of narration. One could probably learn most of what there is to be learned about novel writing, by pulling this one work to bits and then reassembling.

ONE AMERICAN, MODERN, COMIC AND SAD

THE CATCHER IN THE RYE takes us from the mid-nineteeth century into the second half of our own, and from Yorkshire to New York. Salinger's reputation, like Bronte's, rides pretty much on the one novel, which not only became a cult piece in the Swinging Sixties, but also achieved the distinction of getting itself banned in Australia. This, though, was only in the paperback edition; those able to afford hard covers presumably being immune to corruption! The reason for the ban, reportedly, was the call-girl scene. Sixteen year old Holden, in flight from his "phoney" boarding school but disinclined to show up at home, felt so sorry for this girl he'd (almost accidentally!) summoned to his hotel room, that he decided against "doing it"; and, (thinking very fast indeed) explained to her that because he'd had this operation on his clavichord ...!

CATCHER, at the same time comic and sad, is shortish and an easy read. Unfortunately, as with all later twentieth century authors referred to in this GUIDE, copyright constraints make it impossible to quote directly more than the couple of hundred or so words permissible under 'fair dealing'. You will, though, be able to find and read for yourselves the passages and incidents referred to.

ANTIPODEAN SHORT STORY

Katherine Mansfield, a New Zealander who lived some of her life in England, wrote short stories that are, at their best, models of their kind. They can be amusing, poignant, satirical, bitter, ironic. Scenes and character are observed with razor-eye (if there's such a thing!) and rendered vividly and with the greatest economy. We have chosen her collection BLISS, in considerable part because in it she demonstrates how one can coax stories out of just the most everyday material, out of incidents available to absolutely everyone. Most discussion is drawn from the title story, "Bliss", which takes only about twenty minutes to read.

JOB DESCRIPTION

One final point to make in this Introduction; this time, about being a writer, rather than about writing itself.

Being a writer is more than just another job. A real writer never simply puts in the hours, then knocks off. In fact, to choose to be a writer is very definitely to choose a lifestyle! You will find yourself, in a sense, on duty twenty-four hours a day, all your life. Even your dreaming time becomes part of your software! Your subconscious, too, is always on stand-by; is, in fact, probably your managing director! Family, friends, colleagues, everything that you see from the bus window, constitutes your raw material. As for your secret thoughts and fantasies and judgements of people — what the poet Yeats called the rag and bone shop of the heart — all these, too, you will be picking over, as grist for that mill.

One of Chekhov's characters in the play THE SEAGULL remarks that a writer devours his own life. It's all copy — even your shame, guilt, grief, treacheries. Indeed, everything you experience, you actually experience twice. First, you experience it *inside*, just as yourself. At the same time, you also experience it from *outside*, as an observer, distanced, and more objective, impersonal. That is, yourself as a character, behaving in certain ways that you are as a writer witnessing; noting your own motives, ploys, gestures, vulnerabilities, raw points, brutalities, the lot!

These attitudes to writing mostly come gradually, of course; though after a time, pretty much automatically too. Here following are some habits and practices to set up, that will project you into writer-mode and help keep you there for as long as you really want to remain a writer.

Don't despise any kind of professional writing

Do "Letters to the Editor", filler columns, short articles, reviews, reports of local events; and write them for nothing, if nothing's all that's on offer. Such tasks not only keep you 'thinking writing', they make for good practice in ordering material and establishing tone; and of course anything that gets published boosts self-confidence, which can often drop low, low, low!

Write regularly

Sure, a few writers do rely on the intermittent inspirational burst; but most of us need steady production, or we simply drift out of writing. It helps if you have a special room with desk, files, privacy. For one thing, you can leave all your mess there between stints. For another, you'll feel like a writer every time you walk in to that room; and this helps to make you a writer and to keep you one. If, however, all that's available is one end of a kitchen table ... well, our first published book, a biography (for teenagers) of Sir Edmund Hillary of Everest, was written exactly thus! It's the daily stint at your workplace (cleared of toast and coffee cups!), the weekly programme and set quota, that makes one a writer.

Don't look for too much consensus about writing skills

Henry Miller, for example, exhorted writers always to finish one work before beginning another. This might work well for some; but our experience and that of any other writers we know directs to having several projects running concurrently, so that if one dries up ... ? There's also the consideration that if you've only that one sole work on the bench, then when that's finished, all you have left is a vacuum and a whole new start ahead of you. We've *never* been finished, in this sense, in decades!

Keep notes

Have files, notebooks, whatever you call them ... in which you keep plot ideas, character sketches, descriptions of scenes, fragments of dialogue, text for revision or working on — those kinds of things. That way, you'll always have something to do when you move into your writing patch. You'll constantly be 'thinking writing'.

Enjoy your own company

Then perhaps most important of all, remember that as a writer you are the quintessential loner. No one can write for another person any more than they can take over that person's pain or grief or love-making. To be a writer, you have to be self-motivating, self-energising, self-directing, self-propelling and to a considerable degree self-sustaining. It can be lonely indeed, just you, and that desk, and those imperious and yet elusive ideas, and your machine.

A great many students enrolling in creative writing classes drop away after a time; often, after a quite short time. The reason, in the main, is that these students really only *thought* they wanted to be writers. Their dream was not solitariness-proof!

Now let's move to writing quality fiction.

The first chapter will deal with peopling your fiction — how characters get created and managed. Later chapters will provide these characters with a plot that embodies a theme, in a setting, with narration and dialogue, and of course a beginning and an ending. But characters come first, even if, when initially you envisage them, they're already enmeshed in your mind with some prepared story. Because when the plots and themes and settings of fictions grow dim in your recollection, it's the inhabitants, the characters, who remain with you.

How many of us, for example, can remember much of the plots in which Hamlet figures, or Shylock, or Romeo and Juliet, or Frankenstein, or Oliver Twist, or Sherlock Holmes, or James Bond, or Christopher Robin, or Billy Bunter, or Superman, or Donald Duck ...?

2

Characterisation

The foundation of good fiction is character-creating and
nothing else. ... Style counts; plot counts; originality of
outlook counts. But none of these counts anything like so
much as the convincingness of the characters. If the
characters are real the novel will have a chance; if they are
not, oblivion will be its portion.

ARNOLD BENNETT

T here's one widespread misconception about the writing
of fiction. It's that plot is central to any and every story.
Even texts and courses on creative writing have said so.
Plot, however, is not at all what is central to fiction. Character is!
It's not *what* happens; rather, that it's happening to *someone*.
Character revealed in the course of illustrative action, some
would say. So it is with characterisation that we will begin.

Portray vividly an interesting human being, and most of us
will be looking to read about that person. Journalists fill
newspaper and magazine pages with such pieces; and television
similarly; what sort of person that celebrity or tennis player or
judge or victim or villain is; his/her appearance, activities,
ambitions, failures, struggles, opinions.

Here, for example, is Elizabeth, at one o'clock in the morning,
answering her sister's phone call:

"Vicki. Is anything wrong?"

"Not exactly."

"What's the time over there?"

10

"Ten o'clock in the night."

"I can't come over again," said Elizabeth. "I don't know why you're ringing me. The phone bill must be colossal. Have you been going to school?"

"Sort of. Not all that much." ...

"You swore you were old enough to look after yourself. I warned you. I told you I couldn't keep on coming over. Do you know what that air fare costs?"

"I don't want you to come over," said Vicki. Her voice was dull. "I made a mistake. I want to come over there."

"To LIVE?"

"I'm only seventeen."

"Last time we had this discussion, seventeen was adult, remember?"

Very little 'story' here — just two people manoeuvring per phone. But to read it as largely uninhabited plot: these two sisters live on opposite sides of the globe, and one indicates that she wants to return to the other.

Boring? So the example, from Helen Garner's THE CHILDREN'S BACH, precisely encapsulates what is meant by 'illustrative action'. Once you have a real and convincing character, this character will be *doing* something. Cooking a meal ... or the books. Fighting a blizzard ... or temptation. Struggling to reach a decision ... or to resist an erotic encounter. Planning a surprise party; or silently grieving; or just waiting and wondering. The character can be involved in outer doing or inner doing, past doing or projected doing. Whatever, action of some sort will be involved, will be occurring; as with Elizabeth and Vicki's fencing across phone lines.

Even if you try to present a character doing nothing whatsoever — if you restrict yourself, say, to an inventory of dress and physical appearance, you still won't find it easy to avoid this sense of something going on, of action.

George, for example, is in a good but rather rumpled suit, unshaven, hollow eyed, hair tousled. Something unusual, then, will likely need to be explained to somebody? To George's boss? To his partner? Already there's a sense of some explanation required about what has happened; and about what will happen next, when George gets to front up.

Or if you sketch Janey in a boutique gown of Venetian scarlet with Art Deco gold jewellery shimmering like her smooth straight hair and her handbag and her stilted, attenuated shoes? Something portends there too. Janey on the hunt? If so, for what? For whom? If you should happen to find her fashion items all brash or inconsistent one with another; well, one might wonder then about the purposes of a woman with such obvious wealth, but so little understanding of the particular world she has chosen to move in. How will she make out, in such a situation?

What all the above adds up to is this: get some real characters, and they will initiate situations and narrative for you. This will not necessarily be fully fledged plot; but it can hardly be less than a sound basis for generating such plot.

How, then, does one create convincing, incident-sparking characters?

TAGGING

For fairly minor characters, some single 'identifying tag' is usually sufficient. You look for something about the particular person that is both very noticeable, and also seems to sum him/her up; almost a label. Just a sentence or two will often do this for you. Here are two examples we used in WRITE YOUR LIFE — A GUIDE TO AUTOBIOGRAPHY:

> Aunt Matilda could sail into a room, with her majestic hat and imperious brolly, and sweep us all silent with slow survey.

> Though Rupert Mantle was short and slight, he wore his glasses low on the bridge of his nose. At the dining table, his pale blue eyes would glimmer over the tops of his steel rims, and subdue us all entirely.

Each of these characters has the tag 'auctoritas'. Each time one appears, the reader would respond: 'That's the intimidating-eyes one.'

Here are two further examples, from "Bliss":

> And then Miss Fulton, all in silver, with a silver fillet binding
> her pale blonde hair, came in smiling.

There are some theme implications in this tagging of Miss Fulton as "silver", which are discussed in Chapter 4; and she is, of course, a major character in plot terms. The tagging as "silver" seems to suggest enough about her appearance and her nature.

> The bell rang. It was lean, pale Eddie Warren (as usual) in
> a state of acute distress.

> "It is the right house, isn't it?" he pleaded.

> "Oh I think so — I hope so", Bertha said brightly.

> " I have had such a dreadful experience with a taxi-man; he
> was most sinister. I couldn't get him to stop. The more I
> knocked and called the faster he went. And in the
> moonlight this bizarre figure with the flattened head
> crouching over the little wheel ... "

> He shuddered, taking off an immense white silk scarf.
> Bertha noticed that his socks were white, too — most
> charming.

That's tagging the affected aesthete doing-a-simper at the front door. Bertha, by the way, is also being characterised here, by her tacitly-endorsing response to such a stereotype. That is, she hardly recoils in horror or collapses into mirth!

Salinger in CATCHER does tagging with great skill. Mrs Morrow, whom Holden meets on the train, speaks with "a nice telephone voice". Her son, Ernest, was the sort of obnoxious young male who, after showers, went down the corridor flicking a towel at others' behinds. Bob Robinson is the student who's embarrassed by his mother and father's saying "she don't" and "he don't". Holden's teacher, Old Spencer, gets attacks of nodding when listening; and whether he's listening or not, his nose runs. Jane Gallagher, for whom Holden has genuine respect and affection, would never, when playing checkers, move any of her Kings. She'd leave them all lined up in the back row! "She just liked the way they looked, all in the back row." A hat check girl he encounters is simply tagged as "motherly" — she won't take Holden's tip, but makes him put his hat on, because his hair's wet, and urges him to get home and to bed.

More than one single tag is needed to contain Martha, the strident but sorely-troubled academic wife in Edward Albee's WHO'S AFRAID OF VIRGINIA WOOLF? What is perhaps most foregrounded about her in this play, however, is her flight from her sorrows and her fears into alcohol. There is one short drunken speech in the play that, through its dramatic structure and its wildly comic image, conveys this perfectly.

*... you cry all the time, don't you? ... Yes; you do. You cry
alllll the time. ... I cry all the time too. ... but deep inside,
so no one can see me. ... We both cry all the time, and
then, what we do, we cry, and we take our tears, and we
put 'em in the ice box, in the goddam ice trays (Begins to
laugh) until they're frozen (Laughs even more) and then ...
we put them ... in our ... drinks!*

Names can be used for tagging, the name suggesting the tagged quality. Shakespeare, for example, has a wonderful range of prostitutes — Doll Tearsheet, Jane Nightwork, Mistress Overdone and Mistress Quickly. (This latter would have been pronounced Quick Lie!) Dickens too. The low life swindler who got into the big money ... and right out of his depth — Montague Twigg. The predatory, sanctimonious, and disdainful hypocrite — Mr Pecksniff. The grotesque, black-robed widow whose secret of managing children was "to give them everything that they didn't like and nothing that they did" — Mrs Pipchin. The rascally, bouncy factory owner — Mr Bounderby. The nasty little old man who screamed abuse at people from the depths of his great chair and hurled cushions at his deaf and senile wife — Grandfather Smallweed.

For more important characters, however, more substantial characterisation than a simple tag is required. This can be achieved for the most part by extending and deepening those simple tagging devices; as:

➤ Biography

➤ Dress

➤ Physical Appearance

➤ Actions

➤ Dialogue

➤ Surroundings

➤ Beliefs and Values.

And of course, there is *response* to any of these. One character's response to another's actions or dress or values, acts to characterise that 'responder'.

Let's deal with each of the above in turn:

BIOGRAPHY

This can consist simply of a few biographical facts pertinent to the story being told.

> *Aimee had for sixteen years been the central fact and focus of attention for her relatively aged parents. The most spacious nursery room in the suburb; the most genteel and expensive school in the city; as exotic and boutique a wardrobe as had ever featured in the glossiest of glossies. She had passed her sixteen years without serious illness and with very little in the way of frustration generally; and reached a vague sort of conclusion that the Great World Outside rather admired her, and existed in large part to provide her pleasures and general satisfaction.*

Such a broadly biographical introduction to a character could well be followed by plans for an appropriately elaborate world tour to cap such a childhood and adolescence ... or by the sudden death of her parents. Either might produce a good novel. The opening of Jane Austen's EMMA has a strongly biographical component like this, also intimating riding-for-a-fall.

> *Emma Woodhouse, handsome, clever, and rich, with a comfortable home and happy disposition, seemed to unite some of the best blessings of existence; and had lived nearly twenty-one years in the world with very little to distress or vex her.*

Here's another introduction of a central character through biography, from Charles Dickens' GREAT EXPECTATIONS.

> *My father's family name being Pirrip, and my Christian name Philip, my infant tongue could make of both names nothing longer or more explicit than Pip. So, I called myself Pip, and came to be called Pip.*

> I give Pirrip as my father's family name, on the authority of
> his tombstone and my sister — Mrs Joe Gargery, who
> married the blacksmith. As I never saw my father or my
> mother, and never saw any likeness of either of them (for
> their days were long before the days of photographs), my
> first fancies regarding what they were like, were
> unreasonably derived from their tombstones. The shape of
> the letters on my father's, gave me an odd idea that he
> was a square, stout, dark man, with curly black hair. From
> the character and turn of the inscription, "Also Georgiana
> Wife of the Above", I drew a childish conclusion that my
> mother was freckled and sickly. To five little stone lozenges,
> each about a foot and a half long, which were arranged in
> a neat row beside their grave, and were sacred to the
> memory of five little brothers of mine — who gave up
> trying to get a living, exceedingly early in that universal
> struggle — I am indebted for a belief I religiously
> entertained that they had all been born on their backs with
> their hands in their trousers-pockets, and had never taken
> them out in this state of existence.

In each of these examples more is being done, of course, than providing character through elements of biography. While it might be appropriate sometimes to give direct biography only ('Abe Hacker was a sixty-four-year-old born in the Canadian forests who, since leaving school at twelve, had worked only in his father's mill, marrying at ..') it would seem a pity not to use those concurrent opportunities offered for establishing setting, themes, tone and the like.

DRESS

Certainly clothes maketh the (wo)man; and there is much truth in the quip that we are what we wear. Dress formed a part of the characterisation of Eddie Warren, in "Bliss" his "immense white silk scarf" and white socks. Here's Mrs Norman Knight from the same story:

> ... taking off the most amusing orange coat with a
> procession of black monkeys around the hem and up the
> fronts.

This coat suggests a character swept up by the more flamboyant fashions; and a shallow nature too. Whereas quite a different nature is suggested by the jacket in Jessica Anderson's TIRRA LIRRA BY THE RIVER.

> He wore a black jacket and striped pants, and after confirming my pregnancy he sat with his hands folded and questioned me severely about my motives.

For fun, try this one from the fourteenth century Geoff Chaucer. It's largely dress and physical appearance:

> Crul was his heer, and as the gold it shoon,
> And strouted as a fanne large and brode;
> Ful streight and evene lay his joly shode.
> His rode was reed, his eyen greye as goos.
> With Poules wyndow corven on his shoos,
> In hoses rede he wente fetisly.
> Yclad he was ful smal and proprely
> Al in a kirtel of lyght waget;
> Ful faire and thikke been the poyntes set.
> And thereupon he hadde a gay surplys
> As whit as is the blosme upon the rys.

It's a description of a young man-about-Oxford, Absolon; and rendered into modern English (thus, incidentally, losing all its poetic 'singing' quality) reads:

> His hair was curling and shone like gold, and spread out from his head like a large, wide fan! Its parting ran straight and even. His face was florid, his eyes goose-grey. His shoe uppers were carved like the windows of St Paul's Cathedral, and his stockings were elegantly crimson. He was dressed in the most splendid and very latest — a jacket of sky blue, with its laces fine and strong. Over all that, he wore a cape as white as blossom on a bough.

So the Lovely Generation were around even five hundred years back! Chaucer goes on to relate how Pretty Absolon wanders around at night serenading under windows and flirting with bar girls. He comes to an humiliating end (much too bawdy to be detailed here!), and all this flows in considerable part from his character as presented above.

For major characters, you will need more than the one dress appearance. If you know these major characters as well as you should — because they are to underpin your novel — you will be quite confident about what each would wear at a wedding, at a funeral, at work, in the kitchen, gardening, out walking, at the movies, on a picnic, at the beach ... the lot!

PHYSICAL APPEARANCE

This was to some extent covered under dress, which is of course part of physical appearance. A minor example would be Holden's summing up of the bellboy who took him to his hotel room as "one of those bald guys that comb all their hair over from the side" to disguise their baldness. In TIRRA LIRRA BY THE RIVER Jessica Anderson describes her car-driver as "about sixty, tall and ponderous, with a turtle head"; and a doctor as "a short thin sallow man with little faded blue eyes set in huge sockets".

Here is a more complex example, from Alice Walker's THE COLOR PURPLE. The semi-literate black American from the Deep South, Celie, tells of the arrival of the ill but tarted up singer, Shug Avery.

> And she dress to kill. She got on a red wool dress and chestful of black beads. A shiny black hat with what look like chickinhawk feathers curve down side one cheek, and she carrying a little snakeskin bag, match her shoes.
>
> She look so stylish it like the trees all round the house draw themself up tall for a better look. Now I see she stumble ... She don't seem that well acquainted with her feets.
>
> Close up I see this yellow powder caked up on her face. Red rouge. She look like she ain't long for this world but dressed well for the next. But I know better.
>
> Come on in, I want to cry. To shout. Come on in. ...
>
> She got a long pointed nose and big fleshy mouth. Lips look like black plum. Eyes big, glossy. Feverish. And mean. Like, sick as she is, if a snake cross her path, she kill it.
>
> She look me over from head to foot.

What is complex here, of course, is the interweaving of the description of Shug Avery with Cella's response to it. The intruder desperate and in war paint, and the tiny, all-there-is home patch to be defended. In the event, though, it does not actually turn out that way. Shug's illness intervenes, redirects events and alliances.

The first couple of pages of Kay Gregory's A PERFECT BEAST (Mills and Boon) go in quite heavily for characterising per appearance. Here are the fragments:

> Rosemary ran her fingers distractedly through her long, pale-blonde hair ...

> She tossed her hair behind her shoulders and smiled a little defensively ...

> ... her serious little face. When she smiled, the faint freckles which dotted her cheekbones seemed to form into laugh lines to her gold-flecked eyes, and the long curving mouth curled infectiously at the corners.

The main agent of characterisation in this novel as a whole is actually action. Rosemary is presented initially as hurling chalk around her empty classroom, and responds thereafter with fighting spirit to several 'dramas' that hit her.

ACTIONS

That is, your character *doing* something.

It is probably action, both outer and inner action, that most establishes and communicates character. What the character thinks and plans and decides and flinches from, as well as what the character actually does physically.

Action is also probably the easiest method of characterising. If your personae are clearly and plausibly conceived, they will act 'in character' — which in turn, does further characterising for you.

Salinger's Holden Caulfield, for example, relates how the night his young brother Allie died, he smashed every window in the garage with his fist, and tried to smash the new station sedan's windows too, only his hand was by then too injured for him to do so. This (re)action (for which his uncomprehending parents want to have him psychoanalysed!) communicates to us powerfully Holden's immense capacity for affection, as well as the force of his grief and rage.

William Mayne's Parson Ramage (THE JERSEY SHORE) is an equally effective passage of characterisation by action. An old man tells the boy Arthur of an eighteenth century cleric who was much more a man of the fox hunt than a man of God.

> *"Osney, where I was a lad; the parson there. See him, a wild man, devout to hawk and hound, him. Great, tall, broad, lord of the manor, the roaringest man that ever backed horse or beat a sermon through the brake and slew it in a corner of the pulpit. Set to a hound he would any day but Sunday, set it to anything that moved, coney, hare, cat, rat, dog, child or bishop, come it wasn't Sunday. Sundays he allowed God was abroad ready to set archangels on him like hounds. Days of the week Parson Ramage hunted all and sundry; holy days he let loose a bagged sermon, cornered him up, killed him, and slung him a-horseback and travelled him out of church, dead, aye dead..*

This is of course the tagging technique, but it is extended so that Parson Ramage is seen as bringing his essential fox-hunter character into even his clerical duties. The name is a tag too, of course: ramage — rampage — damage. Mayne proceeds to add some account of physical appearance to this tagging above — the parson is big as a tree, with a great red face, and with the hair falling over his forehead hacked short, to keep it out of his eyes when wind is up.

And from CATCHER again: Holden suspects that one of his teachers, Mr Antolini, attempted a "flitty pass" at him. One very particular action of Mr Antolini's, though, restrains Holden from making any harsh final judgement about this teacher. It follows the suicide of James Castle from a high window. While half the school just stand paralysed around the shattered body, Mr Antolini acts. He feels the boy's pulse, then wraps the bloodied corpse in his coat and carries it to the school infirmary.

DIALOGUE

People also proclaim something of their characters through what they say and the ways they say it — to themselves (interior dialogue), as well as to others.

> Glendower : *At my birth, the frame and huge foundation of the earth shaked like a coward.*

Hotspur :	Why so it would have done at the same season if your mother's cat had but kittened.
Glendower :	I say the earth did shake when I was born!
Hotspur:	And I say the earth was not of my mind, if you suppose as fearing you, it shook.
Glendower:	The heavens were all on fire! The earth did tremble!
Hotspur:	O then the earth shook to see the heavens on fire, and not in fear of your nativity.
Glendower:	Cousin — give me leave to tell you *once again*, that at my birth the front of heaven was full of fiery shapes. These signs have marked me EXTRAORDINARY . I am not in the roll of common men.
Hotspur:	I think there's no man speaks better Welsh! I'll to dinner!
Glendower:	I CAN CALL SPIRITS FROM THE VASTY DEEP!
Hotspur:	Why so can I, or so can any man. But will they come when you do call for them?

This exchange (a little editied) is from Shakespeare's HENRY IV Pt I. Through dialogue alone, the touchy, messianic Welsh leader, and his blunt and dismissive English ally, are sharply etched. It hardly bodes well for harmonious co-operation in their joint rebellion against the King!

Talk can also be to a character's own self, or more often, perhaps, to the reader. Indeed, CATCHER is really one long such monologue to this hypothetical reader; and Charlotte Bronte's JANE EYRE is similarly so. For example, the novel opens with Jane plunging straight into an account of her life as a child and an orphan.

> There was no possibility of taking a walk that day. We had been wandering, indeed, in the leafless shrubbery an hour in the morning; but since dinner (Mrs Reed, when there was no company, dined early) the cold winter wind had brought with it clouds so sombre, and a rain so

penetrating, that further out-door exercise was now out of the question.

I was glad of it: I never liked long walks, especially on chilly afternoons: dreadful to me was the coming home in the raw twilight, with nipped fingers and toes, and a heart saddened by the chidings of Bessie, the nurse, and humbled by the consciousness of my physical inferiority to Eliza, John, and Georgiana Reed.

The said Eliza, John, and Georgiana were now clustered round their mama in the drawing room: she lay reclined on a sofa by the fireside, and with her darlings about her (for the time neither quarrelling nor crying) looked perfectly happy. Me, she had dispensed from joining the group; saying, "She regretted to be under the necessity of keeping me at a distance; but that until she heard from Bessie, and could discover by her own observation that I was endeavouring in good earnest to acquire a more sociable and childlike disposition, a more attractive and sprightly manner, — something lighter, franker, more natural as it were — she really must exclude me from privileges intended only for contented, happy, little children."

"What does Bessie say I have done?" I asked.

"Jane, I don't like cavillers or questioners: besides, there is something truly forbidding in a child taking up her elders in that manner. Be seated somewhere; and until you can speak pleasantly, remain silent."

This talking-to-the reader is quite patent in the final chapter, where Jane opens with the famous: "Reader, I married him."; and goes on:

A quiet wedding we had: he and I, the parson and clerk, were alone present.

BELIEFS AND VALUES

What an individual believes in, and holds of value, is very much part of what brings that individual to life as a character. The range of possibilities here is quite wide, and extends from simple tagging, to making the driving force of the novel the beliefs and values of some major character.

For a minor character, you can simply establish a sort of general attitude to life. So, Jade is earnest, or sly, or directs her life by astrology, or spends her days shadow-boxing the memory of her overpowering parents. Brad is aggressive, or car mad, or at sixty is involved in legal actions against almost everyone in his close and extended family! Then, whenever such a character steps onto your page, that's what flashes onto the screen of your reader's mind — the sly one, or the aggressive one, or the one who lives by the stars. That is, you have tagged by a significant, even the major, value.

You can similarly link a character to a particular ideology. Mariellen is the quintessential feminist — or leftie — or greenie — or all three. She could equally well be the quintessential 'redneck', stalking 'grots' and 'queers' and 'dole bludgers'. (Though hardly with the name Mariellen. Perhaps Mrs Augusta Straitem, or Marjorie Lasher?)

These sorts of values-tags — though some are rather more substantial than others — sum up in ways that not only draw attention to what these particular individuals are like in themselves, but also to the nature of the part they will be playing on the pages. Janelle's essential mischievousness will provoke some awful misunderstanding between the main lovers, perhaps. Will's meanness will provoke a family crisis, with teenage Joanna storming out and living the life of a street-kid (which becomes the main matter of the novel?). Mariellen might just have a walk-on part in a novel about a group of greenies who take on the timber industry in a forest confrontation; though in such a case, she'd need some further tagging as her 'greenie-ness' wouldn't distinguish her from others of her crowd. Perhaps she's the greenie with the long gold hair and equally long silences? They're her tags? Or she's the greenie whose parents make great wealth from wood-chipping? Perhaps you will use one or other of these tags, some place in the novel, to nudge the plot this way or that? That is, when she *does* finally speak up? Or when her parents intervene?

The more important characters can likewise have beliefs and values as central to them. An ideology-driven individual could sustain a novel; Cathy Leuwin the human rights lawyer, Colonel Breckon who sees blacks or women's groups or Serbs or Jews or Asians — or even human rights lawyers — as the enemies to be exterminated.

23

If beliefs-and-values is read broadly, it could include the more generally passion-dominated individual. For example, Shakespeare's Macbeth decides that the Scottish crown is worth whatever might be the personal costs of winning it. And Heathcliff elects to live for vengeance. This driven-by-passion is how we see and understand them, and it is what creates or feeds strongly into incidents, and rounds these incidents up into a full plot.

Here are several examples which effectively characterise per the values made evident through them.

The first concerns George, Martha's historian husband in WHO'S AFRAID OF VIRGINIA WOOLF?, who has strong humanist values — civilised values as opposed to barbarism. In response to a contemptuous "Up yours!" from Nick, a shallow biologist on the make, George passionately declaims these values. His speech, as with Martha's earlier, is far from being a straightforward *credo*. Rather, it is dramatic in form, using the devices of rhetoric.

> You take the trouble to construct a civilisation ... to ... to
> build a society, based on the principles of ... principle ...
> you endeavour to make communicable sense out of
> natural order, morality out of the unnatural disorder of
> man's mind ... you make government and art ... you bring
> things to the saddest of all points ... to the point where
> there IS something to lose ... then all at once, through all
> the music, through all the sensible sounds of men
> building, attempting, comes the *Dies Irae*. And what is it?
> What does the trumpet sound? UP YOURS!

There is a scene in George Eliot's THE MILL ON THE FLOSS where Tom and Maggie Tulliver try to come to terms with their father's sudden and serious illness, his likely bankruptcy, their mother's distress and their aunt's censure. Tom and Maggie's responses fetch out their motivations and their values — only some of which they share. Tom in this scene tries to comfort his mother, who is concerned most about losing her own family's "things". Maggie listens a time. Then:

> "Mother, how can you talk so? As if you cared only for
> things with YOUR name on, and not for what has my
> father's name too. And to care about anything but dear
> father himself! — when he's lying there and may never

*speak to us again. Tom, you ought to say so too — you
ought not to let anyone find fault with my father."*

*Maggie, almost choked with mingled grief and anger, left
the room, and took her old place on her father's bed. Her
heart went out to him with a stronger movement than
ever at the thought that people would blame him. Maggie
hated blame: she had been blamed all her life, and
nothing had come of it but evil tempers. Her father had
always defended and excused her, and her loving
remembrance of his tenderness was a force within her that
would enable her to do or bear anything for his sake.*

*Tom was a little shocked at Maggie's outburst — telling
HIM as well as his mother what it was right to do! She
ought to have learned better than have those hectoring,
assuming manners by this time. But he presently went into
his father's room and the sight there touched him in a way
that effaced the slighter impressions of the previous hour.
When Maggie saw how he was moved, she went to him
and put her arm round his neck as he sat by the bed, and
the two children forgot everything else in the sense that
they had one father and one sorrow.*

The final example for beliefs-and-values is another complex,
even poetical, one, where the values reside implicitly rather than
gain explicit expression. In it, Holden Caulfield (CATCHER)
meditates on his own death, then progresses laterally, per
cemeteries, to his brother, Allie's death; and those things that he
considers important, and those that he does not, become very
clear indeed.

He ponders first about his mother wondering what to do with
all his clothes and sports gear if he'd died; and then about "the
whole bunch of them sticking me in a goddam cemetery and all",
with his name on a tombstone and "dead guys" all around and
flowers on his stomach on Sundays. ("Who wants flowers when
you're dead?") He then transfers to Allie's grave, which his parents
visit. Holden no longer accompanies them. It's not so bad on
sunny days, he explains; but when it rains, on Allie's "lousy
tombstone ... on the grass on his stomach", all the cemetery
visitors can run to their cars and listen to their radios or go "some
place nice" to eat. All except Allie, that is. Holden acknowledges
that it's "only his body and all" in the earth; but he still cannot

bear it. "You didn't know him. If you'd known him, you'd know what I mean. It's not too bad when the sun's out, but the sun only comes out when it feels like coming out."

SURROUNDINGS

This is characterising individuals by their 'space', if they have made this space at least to some extent personally theirs; put their own imprint on their room or whatever. For example, Johnno's father in JOHNNO:

> *Wearing a leather apron and shorts, with his tool box open on the bench behind him, all its bits and chisels neatly stacked, and a stub of a pencil behind his ear, he would work for long hours in the gloom under the house ...*

Bertha's space in "Bliss" is quite a different kind of room:

> *Mary brought in the fruit on a tray and with it a glass bowl, and a blue dish, very lovely, with a strange sheen on it as though it had been dipped in milk.*
>
> *"Shall I turn on the light, M'm? "*
>
> *"No, thank you. I can see quite well."*
>
> *There were tangerines and apples stained with strawberry pink. Some yellow pears, smooth as silk, some white grapes covered with a silver bloom and a big cluster of purple ones. These last she had bought to tone in with the new dining-room carpet. Yes, that did sound rather far-fetched and absurd, but it was really why she had bought them. She had thought in the shop: I must have some purple ones to bring the carpet up to the table. And it had seemed quite sense at the time.*
>
> *When she had finished with them and had made two pyramids of these bright round shapes, she stood away from the table to get the effect — and it really was most curious. For the dark table seemed to melt into the dusky light and the glass dish and the blue bowl to float in the air. This, of course in her present mood, was so incredibly beautiful. ... She began to laugh.*

Other forms of characterising are going on here too — through action, and indeed through tone; but space is probably the most effective instrument of characterisation at this point?

Here, from W.J. Burley's WYCLIFFE AND THE DUNES MYSTERY is Molly Bissett, quite straightforwardly presented through dress, physical appearance and surroundings:

> (The house) was set well back from the road with a
> gravelled drive and laurel hedges, a four-square house with
> a squat hipped roof and overhanging eaves. The lady
> herself answered his ring. She was on the short side,
> inclined to plumpness, dark, with smooth clear skin, and
> features set in a mould of good humour. She wore a
> snugly fitting cherry-coloured jumper with black trousers.
>
> "Do come in."
>
> The drawing room was large, shabby and comfortable,
> with a random assortment of furniture that had seen
> better days. A black and white border collie, sprawled on
> the hearthrug, regarded him with a lazy eye. There was an
> electric fire burning on the hearth, and an open book on
> the floor by the chair in which Molly now sat herself.

Rooms, of course, are only one of the places folk inhabit. You can communicate character by documenting the kinds of shop where you would be likely to find particular people — Mac always calling in to a hardware store, Florrie forever pushing a supermarket trolley, Ebony more likely to be with the boutique clothing. (Does she hunt out sales and discounts, though; or buy without even glancing at the price ticket? Perhaps where she shops they don't even have anything so vulgar as a price ticket? Whatever — it would illuminate Ebony's character.)

One garden shed has neatly stacked shelves, implements hanging from brackets and drawers tagged; while another simply has everything heaped on the floor or stuffed indiscriminately on shelves. Likewise two kitchens — you fill in the details! And cars — one inhabits these too. A basic model, battered, filled with litter; an American import, huge and glittering, with oversized tyres and golden-fleece seat covers with Aztec trinkets and stickers from all over the US.

Even a character's association with locale holds significance.

Rockie hangs round those streets where drugs are pushed and street-kids flaunt sex; whereas Natalie gets associated with wetlands — her boots, her binoculars, her 4WD.

An individual's attitude to his/her surroundings will suggest character too. Dorota (whom we ought maybe to introduce to Natalie?) is never more content than when alone in the bush, striding some forest trail. Jeremy has to meet someone for a pub lunch, and grumbles and grouches about that particular kind of space: he detests the noise and the roughness and the mass produced food. (It wouldn't be hard to give Jeremy a wardrobe of clothes, just from this reaction to this particular space. He certainly wouldn't be an overalls man; and if he were in jeans, they'd be designer and the rest of him impeccable?)

You could have a bombastic politician who is terrified of flying — using aircraft as surroundings. You could even have your whole novel revolve around a character who is fighting to win or preserve a particular surrounding, or to escape from one. That is characterising, and generating plot, all in one! Dealing with a terrorist threat to bomb a particular building or monument would be an example of the first; a gaol or prison camp or (as with the child Jane in Charlotte Bronte's JANE EYRE) a hateful home, of the second.

Use of the techniques outlined above will give you well realised characters — that is, visually rendered and fully recognisable. For compelling fiction, however, such characters must have motivation. As has been indicated several times already in this chapter, it is motivation that drives characterisation into plot.

MOTIVATION

This refers to that inner force which drives a person to want certain things in certain ways; and it is what most fully individualises your character. In its general sense, motivation is what makes those characters dress and speak in the way they do. It is motivation in a specific sense, in relation to some particular issue or cause or event, which creates the plot. Shakespeare certainly understood this; which is perhaps one of the reasons his works have survived the centuries and spread out into other languages and cultures. As:

➢ Macbeth: Ambition

➢ Othello: (Sexual) possession

➢ Hamlet: Justice.

These, of course, are greatly over-simplified. Macbeth's assassinations are also a product of his relationship with his wife — she hungers to be queen, and goads him on. Othello is also confronted with his outsider status — he's a dark and 'savage' Moor in white and 'civilised' Venice, and the victim of a cunning and implacable villain. And Hamlet is intelligent enough to realise that even if his uncle King Claudius did murder his, Hamlet's, father, a retributive slaughter wouldn't exactly address the situation either politically or morally.

What happens in all these is that a character with some strong motivation, comes up against great impediment(s); and this is what precipitates plot for you. It is the degree of motivation, and the degree of resistance from the impediment(s), that contribute most, probably, to strength of plot.

To give individuals such hefty motivation isn't difficult.

What we all want is for the most part simple and naked — food, shelter, wealth, love and lust, status, possessions, power, respect, protection, security; and for some of us, fame, revenge and the like. Hundreds of thousands of tales have been told, for instance, simply about the pursuit of love; from comic to tragic, from Pulp to High Culture's most revered literature. An equal number would have had a protagonist motivated not so much to gain, as to avoid — say, an aircraft crash; or an invasion of earth from outer space; or the murder of a young woman who is, ignorant of her danger, wandering somewhere in a city; or the poisoning of the sacred well by hostile elvelings from Glyph Wood.

Heathcliff's motivation in WUTHERING HEIGHTS could hardly be more powerful or more visible. He wants Catherine; and subsequently he wants vengeance. Add to this the quite primal motivations of several other characters in that novel, and it's hardly surprising one gets such a human earthquake.

It would be worthwhile going through several novels you know well and think highly of, and check out what motivations have been given to the more important characters there. You will find, probably, that many are obviously strong, like jealousy and love and hatred and pursuit of wealth and ideology and craving for glory. Others will not be so obvious, not in such primary colours; but if you search the behaviours closely, you'll certainly find some strong motivation. Otherwise, the characters' actions and their lives would be of little interest to you.

As already stated, what one most needs with a strongly motivated character, is an equally strong impediment to that character reaching his/her goal. It's the irresistible force meeting the immoveable object that creates drama, and will manufacture more plot than you'll ever be able to cope with!

One of the best impediments you can have, is another strongly motivated character in opposition. Heathcliff certainly has one; and it's not so much Edgar or Hindley or Hareton, as Catherine his beloved. She's the one who defies him — by marrying Edgar; and then again, in a way, by dying. On her deathbed, Heathcliff tells her exactly this. (We quoted the passage in Chapter 7.)

With CATCHER, the specific impediment is less clearly adumbrated. It is, in a way, his society which deflects Holden — its "phoniness". He sees his schoolfellows' preying on girls; he experiences a trusted teacher's "flitty" advances; is dismayed by his brother's "prostitution" of his talent by writing for Hollywood; and by his friend Sally Hayes turning into "the queen of the phonies". He is too fundamentally decent to grow into all this without resistance and a troubled spirit. Perhaps, too, there is within Holden a fear of confronting *any* world that would involve taking responsibility for his own life? The divided self can provide very strong motivation and impediment, as many a Russian novelist has realised and exploited.

Here are just a few simple and fairly obvious motivation-with-impediment examples:

Motivation	**Possible Impediment**
To kill John Spee	The bodyguard. Moral scruples. Friendship and affection. Fear of discovery.
To uncover the killer of John Spee	Absence of clues. Threat ex killer.
To wed Juliet	Feuding families violently oppose the marriage.
To wed Mr Rochester	Mr R. already *has* a wife (Mad, and imprisoned in the attic!)

These are, again, somewhat oversimplified; but the bones of the situation are there.

It is, then, this tension between character motivation, and impediment to it, that charges the action of a novel. Indeed, if you know well the area you plan to write about — heart area, as well as physical area — and you have strongly motivated characters opposed by unyielding impediments, the tale should pretty much write itself.

You know Ted well enough to be aware of what he will do when he finds out that Jan has ...; and what Jan's response to that will be ...; and Ted's response, in turn, to that. Roger can come into Ted's story too, character-and-impediment driven. Perhaps Roger is what 'Jan has', and is Ted's impediment? Anyway, when all these characters and motivations strike those walls of impediment, of obstruction — your novel hits climax. Roger sells all Jan's shares. Or Ted gets arrested/knocked unconscious/ dropped from the team/kidnapped/bankrupted/ abandoned for Roger ... which all-in-all should give Ted a day he's unlikely to forget!

We inhabit a cosmos, though, that ignores all fairness; and this can manifest itself in a situation which many an established writer has suffered — that the more well constructed your characters are and the more potently you have motivated them, the more likely you are to strike the problem of one or more of these characters rebelling against you, refusing to do in the plot what you had planned they should do. That is, you've plotted them into action that doesn't really flow from the character traits you've given them.

Or conversely, they want to take over your novel and head it out into their own directions; or simply resign from it, after finding your plot has abandoned them. Mark Twain, the American novelist who wrote TOM SAWYER and HUCKLEBERRY FINN, has an amusing account of how he went about dealing with several characters who proved eventually supernumerary to his novel:

> When the book was finished and I came to look around to
> see what had become of the team I had originally started
> with — Aunt Patsy Cooper, Aunt Betsy Hale, the two boys,
> and Rowena the light-weight heroine — they were nowhere
> to be seen; they had disappeared from the story some time

or other. I hunted about and found them — found them stranded, idle, forgotten, and permanently useless. It was very awkward. It was awkward all round, but more particularly in the case of Rowena, because there was a love match on, between her and one of the twins ... and I had worked it up to a blistering heat and thrown in a quite dramatic love-quarrel, wherein Rowena scathingly denounced her betrothed for getting drunk ... Yes, here she was, stranded with that deep injustice of hers torturing her poor torn heart.

I didn't know what to do with her. I was as sorry for her as anybody could be, but the campaign was over, the book was finished, she was side-tracked, and there was no possible way of crowding her in, anywhere. I could not leave her there, of course. After spreading her out so, and making such a to-do over her affairs, it would be absolutely necessary to account to the reader for her. I thought and thought, and studied and studied; but I arrived at nothing. I finally saw plainly that there was really no way but one — I must simply give her the grand bounce. It grieved me to do it, for after associating with her so much I had come to kind of like her after a fashion, notwithstanding she was such an ass and said such stupid, irritating things and was so nauseatingly sentimental. Still, it had to be done. So (I began) Chapter XVIII with:

Rowena went out in the back yard after supper to see the fireworks and fell down the well and got drowned.

It seemed abrupt, but I thought maybe the reader wouldn't notice it, because I changed the subject right away to something else. Anyway it loosened up Rowena from where she was stuck and got her out of the way, and that was the main thing. It seemed a good prompt way of weeding out people that had got stalled, and a plenty good enough way for those others; so I hunted up the two boys and said *they went out back one night to stone the cat and fell down the well and got drowned.* Next I searched around and found old Aunt Patsy Cooper and Aunt Betsy Hale where they were aground, and said *they went out the back one night to visit the sick and fell down the well and got drowned.*

*I was going to drown some of the others, but I gave up the
idea, partly because I believed that if I kept that up it
would arouse attention ... and partly because it was not a
large well and would not hold any more anyway.*

Finally, characterisation is one area where you can do
'exercises' profitably; indeed, practice is probably as important
here as is know-how. Part of your writing 'assets', then, should be
a Character Folder in which you 'collect characters', both from
real life around you and from fiction you read.

In 'real life around you' you observe people, jotting down
items about them that stand out and suggest the kinds of people
they essentially are. You could resort to the heads already used in
this chapter — physical appearance, dress, etc. Many of the
characters gathered in this way, you would expect in due course
to use. A number of them might generate plot for you. Don't
forget that you can render these characters from their minds or
feelings, that is from inside; or from outside, through the eyes of
others, including that special 'other', the author.

Those characters you collect 'from fiction' you might also use
sometimes; reconstituted, of course, and in new situations of your
creation. You could copy or photocopy for your folder, lines
about them, noting and absorbing the ways in which each
character is being communicated and employed.

Over the course of this century many writers of both novels
and drama have felt unhappy about providing single and simple
motivations to their characters, claiming that in the 'real world'
people act from a whole swag of (often incompatible)
motivations.., or change their motivation(s) as they go along, or
conceal their real motivations, even from themselves.
Characterising in this mode, though, is tricky; and unless you feel
really impelled to try it, best to stay with the more traditional
methods.

3

Plot

In tragic life, God wot,
No villain need be! Passions spin the plot ...

MODERN LOVE George Meredith

A s we've noted, many assume that if you plan to write a
short story or a novel, what you have first to do is get
yourself a plot. After all, characters and setting can
hardly exist in a vacuum — the characters doing nothing but
existing, or the setting empty of anything happening in it.

What strikes, though, about the following passage?

> *She had dreams then. But they got lost along the way.*
> *Sixteen years is a long time. For dreams to stay alive. And it*
> *wasn't as if the dream was to be a Trambert, a Mrs*
> *Trambert, no. Just to have a whole house with her own bit*
> *of land under her feet that she and Jake and their kids*
> *could call their own. But nothing like a few hidings — from*
> *the man sposed to be part of the dream ...*

Not much plot. Mainly, Beth Heke vividly presented through
her thoughts, her dreams, her very identifiable voice. Not even
any physical description. Yet the passage from ONCE WERE
WARRIORS undoubtedly engages and holds reader attention
through the force of inner character action; which, in turn, moves
into plot. On the other hand, as already instanced, plot *without*
character?

> *X loves Y, but Y decides to marry Z who is wealthier.*
> *Whereupon X wreaks vengeance on Y and Z, and also on A,*
> *B, C, D, and E by marrying A to C and B to D and turning F*
> *into an uncouth servant.*

34

This hardly makes for riveting reading. It is, though, pretty much the plot outline for WUTHERING HEIGHTS!

CHARACTER-DRIVEN PLOT

The most important statement to be made about plotting, then, is something of a reiteration — that to be successful, plot must be or must seem to be, character driven. The action(s) of the plot must derive convincingly from the characters.

This character-driving can operate either directly or indirectly.

It operates directly if you take several well realised characters, put them together in some challenging situation, and let them work out where it all goes from there. This is probably what occurs in Arthur Miller's powerful drama THE CRUCIBLE. Miller takes a sixteenth century New England town, Salem, where religion is all-powerful and the inhabitants are riven by feuds and greed. He lets loose a Witch Hunt. This really does sort out the town's individuals; into those who run with church and court in naming and hanging the alleged witches, for reasons psychotic or opportunistic; and those who oppose the hunt, usually with more admirable motives. Characters thrown into a crucible ... and the heat of events turned up on them. The Salem folk respond to this testing-by-fire as their individual characters determine.

This character-driven mode for plot can also operate less directly. That is, you actually start with some rudimentary plot outline, and then devise characters to fit into this outline. Characters whose actions and responses could reasonably be expected to trigger off just such a sequence of events and complications as you've in fact plotted. Indeed, some would see THE CRUCIBLE as fitting this method rather more than the 'directly' mode, in that Miller had an actual historical event to work from, with court records and such. Whatever — there is certainly in the play an enormously strong sense of the characters writing their own script, in response to the Witch Hunt's threats or opportunities.

Most writers would work with this second, less direct, method — that is, from some sort of plot skeleton to begin with. As: "I'll write a story about a woman who, last century, was wrecked on the Queensland coast, preserved by a tribe of Aborigines, and finally restored to civilisation by a runaway convict." This is, in fact, the plot of Patrick White's A FRINGE OF LEAVES; and as he based his novel on the experiences of one Eliza Fraser, one can only assume that basic plot situation, in this sense, came first. It would be apparent to any reader, though, that a deal of work has subsequently gone into characterisation, as character seems to spin out much of the plot, either by initiating action or by reacting (to the storm and wreck, say) in character-determined ways.

The danger with plot-first stories — stories about X, Y and Z, with the actual characters to be filled in later — is that they might end up uninteresting. (Well, who can get really fussed about the fates of X, Y and Z?) And unconvincing, because the characters are not behaving like people we've known but like puppets on strings, with some Great Puppeteer jiggling these strings to fulfil plot requirements. Where such tales do get published, they tend to prove, after the first reading, very forgettable, because once the reader knows *what happens next* and *what happened finally*, there's little else to command attention. Action-packed fiction runs these risks — Westerns and thrillers and mysteries and pulp romances. More ample characterisation, though, keeps novels evergreen, as, for instance, with those featuring richly rendered investigator characters like Hercule Poirot and Miss Marple and Lord Peter Wimsey and Roderick Alleyn and Edmund Campion and Detective Chief Superintendent Wycliffe, and Masters and Green, and Adam Dalgliesh, and several dozen others well known to Crime Club aficionados. These are vivid, credible, individuals who deal with situations in their own very recognisable ways, shaped by their own particular qualities and values.

GOOD CHARACTERISATION, INDIFFERENT PLOTTING

The reverse of strong-plot-but-wooden-characters — that is, good-characterisation-but-indifferent-plotting — seems to work rather better. The clumsy novel, or movie, or play, which nevertheless gives you strongly wrought individuals, is much more likely to hold you in the reading/viewing and leave you with something substantial. George Eliot's THE MILL ON THE FLOSS is an example. For chapter after chapter, not a great deal seems to happen. Aunts and uncles all sit around talking, characters are dealt with in considerable detail. Then in the last few chapters, everything seems to happen at once! But largely because of George Eliot's characters, Maggie and Tom Tulliver, and her penetrating recreation of the provincial life of her area and time, generations continue to read and weep over this imperfect but enduring novel.

MECHANICAL PLOTS

George Eliot, though, was careful to link character to plot. Dickens, on the other hand, was probably over-dependent on plotting. He certainly put an enormous amount of planning into getting them intricate and (melo)dramatic, probably because the novels had to go on, issue after issue, in serial form.

He would divide a broadsheet into columns vertical and horizontal where all the events and characters and other items were slotted and moved about; and he'd write from this. This is likely why the first halves of his novels make better reading, when he was establishing character and setting. Sooner or later though he had to get through those mechanical plots; and this seems to take over the latter halves of the novels, with characters being manipulated and pushed round to fit. Perfection in the marrying of plot to character can be seen, perhaps, in several of the novels of Jane Austen; particularly with PRIDE AND PREJUDICE and EMMA.

All this is by way of making the point that to write a novel isn't simply to string together a number of happenings along a Time Line. It is much more the recording and the communicating of the interactions between people, and between people and events. Such interactions in turn generate further events; to which the characters involved once more react. Proaction, too, has its role in such a series of knock-on situations. That is, the character who kick-starts, rather than reacts to. Darren *will* have Lucy, even if he has to kidnap her to have her. Polly Garden *will* have ... even if she has to sleep with every Councillor to get it!

PLOTS AND STORY

All that said, you do need a plot. First, though — to differentiate plot from story — for the two don't entirely overlap. Plot is more what gives pattern or design, and particularly, a sense of causality, to events that are, on their own, simply story. As the novelist E.M. Forster famously wrote: " 'The king died and the queen died' is a story. 'The king died and then the queen died of grief' is a plot." Plot provides the answers to the *Why?* or *What?* about events in the original story line. These considerations needn't bother us a lot. It is just important to realise that a series of events is not in itself a plot. The events must be linked, interrelated, usually through cause and effect.

So — you need a plot. Here are several ways of getting one:

PLOTTING FROM CHARACTER

Much of this we've covered already. Many writers do it intuitively. For example, that teacher years back who took such a dislike to Little You and lost no opportunity of humiliating you ... then finally suicided and left great wealth to ... Little You? Or to the National War Museum? Or to a hostel for abused children? Anyway, a novel around that troubled, so-destructive character? His/her war experiences perhaps? Romances? Abused childhood? Simply a nasty human being whose unexpected curtain was a product of confusion or deception rather than of any remorse? Whatever, an interesting character expanding into a novel?

Hence, BILLY BATCHELOR, Shirley McLaughlin's successful first novel, had its genesis in her mother's life. (Her mother's radio programme was probably the first such by a woman in Australia, though this particular item didn't get into the novel.) Much of that novel is fiction; but the mother's character generates and pervades a deal of it too, and many of the accompanying incidents and relationships are substantially factual.

So ... you might take for your initiating characters four girlfriends; or an Aboriginal family; or a young constable. All fully known and understood by you. Then put them in situations where they are forced to respond. The four girlfriends all in love with the same man, say, or competing for the same much coveted job. The Aborigines suddenly forced to move, with their children, to some crime-and-alcohol-ridden slum or shanty town. The young constable discovering that his Super. is actually one of the Mr Bigs of the heroin trade. What your characters would do in these situations is hardly for you to decide; it is already programmed into them, if you have realised them well enough. They'll take off on their own and roll plot out for you.

PLOT FROM SITUATION OR INCIDENT

This has been called the *What if ...?* plot spinner. It will allow you to manufacture more plot outlines in a day, probably, than you'll be able to write up in a lifetime. You just look around at anything that's going on, and ask of it: *What if ...?*

So, from the front verandah where this very rudimentary first draft of the present chapter is being scribbled, can be seen a youngish man who is hand-holding a child up steps. Now: *What if* he's abducting that child? From its mother? Why? Alcoholism in the mother? A psychiatric problem? *What if* it's a kidnapping? So cool — the kidnapper just leading the child away from its magnate father on the nearby beach? What might be the purposes of such a kidnapping? Money — or political? *What if* the child just came up to the young man and said: 'My mummy's asleep on that seat/under those bushes and she won't wake up'? Or: 'My father said to ask you to phone the number on this piece of paper and do it quickly or he'll be dead.'? Indeed, *what if* while we are looking at this pair, the child simply starts screaming; or the man picks him up and runs with a pair of police officers or an African elephant in pursuit; or the child suddenly vanishes although there is no cover whatsoever anywhere near; or the man and boy become on the instant woman and girl, or even two dogs. Or there's a newsflash that a father and son claiming to have time-travelled from the Middle Ages were released from hospital before blood tests, just to humour them, revealed they were carrying the Black Death? Or, and finally, *what if* one's partner brings a cup of tea out onto the verandah, glimpses that couple, turns deadly white with the cup crashing to the floor, races to the garage and hurls the car through all the beach traffic ...?

You see, if it's simply plot that's holding you up — stop hypertensing! It should be noted, though, that by far the greater number of plots you'd generate this way, you'd not want to write about. They would not interest you enough to sustain your attention through the long haul of producing a novel. Or they'd take you into areas you are unfamiliar with, like police procedure or medical science. But for plots you are more likely to be able to use, apply the *What if ... ?* to areas that do interest you and which you know something about; and keep each turn or step within those areas of interest and familiarity — nursing, or dreams, or life in minority cultures, or motorcycle racing, or parenting, or ten pin bowls, or dancing, or accountancy, or supermarkets, or the drag-drug-and-AIDs scene. All these areas, by the way, have been used this present year by students in Stott's College creative writing courses. The supermarket background novel, and the short story set amongst drag-drug-and-AIDs characters, are of a standard that makes their publication quite possible.

This *What if ?* ploy is in fact one used in the Stott's novel writing course. Students successfully build plot after plot with it.

Once you have a promising *What if ...?* plot, you've then to turn what is no doubt a pretty bare story line, into a complex of events and settings and character interactions and dialogue and chapters and ... and... This is probably the point at which most novelists do in fact begin — thinking of plot, characters and setting all much at the same time. Credible characters for the events and actions, and (the flip side) credible actions and events for those characters to initiate and perform.

SUB-PLOT

That is, a smaller, supporting plot additional to the main plot and accompanying it throughout the story. You would need, of course, to have some measure of main plot to start with, before sub-plot can actually generate further material for you. You would also need to want to use one or more sub-plots. Not all novels do carry them.

Sub-plots, when employed, seem to perform either or both of two functions. They interact with the main plot, bounce off it, and so generate further plot. And/or they help spell out themes and issues and situations, usually by restating in some way those themes and situations that feature in the main plot.

Plot interaction of this kind might work for you in a detective story, for example, by having John Stannon at the country house when L.L. Strade, the American special envoy, is murdered. All the evidence points to Lucinda, of whom John is enamoured. So while Detective Superintendent Wade tries to build up a case against Lucinda, John sets out to uncover the real murderer and at the same time win his beloved. Thus you have a murder plot and a love plot in tandem; and the things John does will cut across

D.S. Wade's investigations and so create incidents there — angry exchanges or confusions or misdirections. Without the love plot, the murder plot would have headed in quite another and likely much more straightforward direction.

In WUTHERING HEIGHTS, the love story of Hareton and the younger Catherine could be seen as a secondary plot. It has some measure of independent existence from the main Heathcliff/Cathy 1 plot — indeed, it develops and runs its course almost in defiance of that primary love plot, in that a part of Heathcliff's vengeance for his loss of Catherine is his campaign to degrade and brutalise Hareton. In fact, if you employ the term 'love story' widely enough, you find that this novel is a conglomerate of love stories, from Lockwood's flirting at a seaside resort, to Edgar and Catherine, Hindley and Frances, Isabella and Heathcliff, and Linton Heathcliff and the younger Catherine. Each one of these, as sub-plot, has impact on the main love plot.

For example:

➤ Frances' death sends Hindley to drink and hence to even greater brutality against Heathcliff; which in turn impels Heathcliff more towards Catherine and, in due course, to vengeance.

➤ The impact of Edgar's love for Catherine is almost impossible to overstate, as it was the marriage that followed in part from this, that precipitated Heathcliff's U-Turn and hurtled the novel in its trajectory of destruction.

➤ And then it was Heathcliff's constantly viewing the Hareton/younger Catherine love; the realisation that all his striving towards vengeance had produced, finally, was this happy conclusion; that precipitated his, Heathcliff's, decline and death.

As you might expect, Shakespeare was most adept at using sub-plot. If you hold Prince Hal's preparation-for-kingship as the central story of Shakespeare's HENRY IV PT 1, then this main plot is virtually composed of three sub-plots, each characterised by a location. There's the 'battlefield', where King Henry is trying to put down the rebellion of Hotspur and Glendower. There's the 'Court', where he has to deal with a crown not legitimately gained and with a son, Prince Hal, run wild. There is the 'tavern', where this Prince roisters with drunkards and petty thieves and prostitutes.

These three plots really do charge one another. The reason the rebels are defeated, for example, is that Hal repents his wild behaviour and returns to the Court to gather and successfully lead his father's forces on the battlefield. And Hal's low-life tavern experiences have left him with an understanding of the common people and an affection for them, so that on his father's death he is able to offer the riven and battered nation a King for all its citizens.

The message from all the above, then, is this. If you're having trouble getting a main plot to develop and fill out, try harnessing it to a sub-plot, with characters crossing back and forth from one to the other. That should spark a good deal more incident and clash.

BORROWING A PLOT

One final way to get yourself a plot is the most obvious of all — take somebody else's! This isn't as nefarious as it sounds, and it will not bring you to where you get remissions for good behaviour. In fact you needn't even feel embarrassed about it: Shakespeare and Chaucer nicked a great many of their plots; and in Chaucer's case would have been proud to have done so — there was acclaim for doing an old story well or even better!

Here's what's meant:

You read a story about Kerry, a young man rich, selfish, living entirely for sensation and immediate gratification. He finds himself with a group lost on a glacier, or besieged in a village in wartime Vietnam, or in some other way with an isolated and threatened group. The incidents of the story gradually bring this Kerry to see himself for what he is, and isn't; and also to see in his companions those admirable qualities he'd disregarded or despised. So he experiences metamorphosis, and emerges a changed man ... perhaps winning Dee as a result, if there is also in the novel a romance-not-prospering sub-plot.

Now what you can do here is take to bits the successful novel plot (and of course setting and characters) and replace each bit with one of your own. Keep the young male brat or replace with a female equivalent, or go more distant and make the protagonist an older person. Whatever, that core quality of self-centredness and shallowness is retained. Change the setting that provides the initial challenge — a lifeboat from a burning cruise ship, for example; or more distant again, a Board of Directors under threat from Mafia, or from a totalitarian government that wants poison gas manufactured.

Make a start replicating the novel's incidents in your new setting and context, to the extent that they can be so transposed. You will likely find that before too long your incidents start to take on their own momentum anyway. Stake out similar support characters in the same way; and perhaps get Penny in as The Lovely waiting in the wings for just such a personal transformation as Rocky is going to experience. Do all this, and you've developed a sound plot from someone else's; doing little more, really, than transplanting the structure and the patterns underlying events; and of course learning somewhat about how-to-plot in the process.

It has been noted from way back what you will likely have decided for yourself — that in all literature there is really only a handful of basic plots. Skill in plotting then lies very much in how these bare-bones are fleshed out and transformed by new bits-of-business, and of course by character action.

CHRONOLOGY

One final point now about plotting — chronology. That is, where events will go along the Time Line of your novel.

Obviously, the events that make up your plot will have occurred one after the other — a first event, then a second, a third: Monday, Tuesday, Thursday, Sunday week. It can't happen otherwise, unless you're writing a Time Machine novel! You might have 159 such events; and as events in the real world they will necessarily have run from 1 to 159, in order.

This obvious point is stressed so it will be very clear what is meant by stating that these events, as you record and report them in your novel, don't at all have to follow that real-world Time Line. You can start with Event 77, then move to Event 35 and to Event 26. You could even start with Event 159, which is the last one, and finish with Event 1!

But why would you ever want to mess about with a Time Line in such a way?

Many a novel does in fact begin with an event that is either the final one or close to it. A body floating in a river. An old man weeping on a park bench. A young man walking up steps with a child by the hand, observed by a scribbler from a front verandah. And then the novel goes back to, say, Event 1, and takes you along the Time Line to the penultimate event. At which point, you will have come to know exactly *How* and *Why* that floating body ..., or that old man weeping, ... or that man and child on the steps ...

The Flashback is one particular way the actual Time Line of events gets chopped about. It occurs when the sequence of the events is being followed for the most part, but (probably) has not begun with Event 1 but with, say, Event 10. Every now and then, therefore, the narrative movement forward is checked, while one of those earlier, pre-10 events, is fed in. Movies do this a great deal.

WUTHERING HEIGHTS is about as complex an example of Time Line rearrangement as you're likely to find. The novel opens when its events have in fact run the greater part of their course - with the visit of Mr Lockwood to "Wuthering Heights" some twenty years after the death of the first Catherine and when Heathcliff's own decease is drawing near. Lockwood experiences there so strong a sense of a mysterious and violent past, that he sets about trying to uncover it.

Most of the novel's pages after this opening event deal with what has in fact already happened. This what-has-already-happened is, in its turn, communicated to us in only the very loosest of time sequences, because Lockwood's and Nellie's narration actually jumps around a good deal on the Time Line; to this-event and that-event-before-it and that-event-after-it. All this is further scrambled by the fact that some of the latter sections of the story are actually going on while the narrators are immersed in what went before; and there is of course still some future story to be incorporated. Indeed one might expect such a kitchen-whizz treatment of chronology to provide a reader with a hopeless task, trying to sort out what exactly is, and has been, going on. That there is no such confusion, testifies to Bronte's very great skill.

This challenging chronology seems to have a purpose that is plot related. It enables Emily Bronte to present to us *together*, two facets of Heathcliff that occur well separated on that Time Line — the brutal and remorseless avenger, and the passionate lover, weeping anguished tears at a snow-driven window. We also see juxtaposed, equally early on, Heathcliff's sullen bullying of Hareton and the second Catherine; and from the first Catherine's journal, the gentle and affectionate child who'd wandered the moors peacefully with that Catherine.

The effect of this on readers, almost certainly, is that later in the novel, when we learn of the enormities Heathcliff perpetrates (and perpetrates mainly on women and children!) most of us do not completely lose sympathy for him? We remember something of what we discovered first up — that before Heathcliff became a monster, he was himself brutally abused. Before he inflicted so much suffering, he had great suffering inflicted on him. Before he became villain, he was victim: We know also how overwhelming was his love for Catherine; and that it has never wavered, even over the long twenty years since her death. And that we know all this, and so retain some sympathy for demonic Heathcliff, is largely because Emily Bronte chose to begin her novel as and where she did, with her Time Line so scrambled.

One last point about chronology. You don't have to work out in advance the order in which you will present the events of your novel. You can quite readily begin *writing* your story at that story's beginning-in-time, at Event 1; then write Event 2, and so on, up to 159. After all that has been done, you can then consider any shuffling around of the order of these events, with whatever linkings and bits of filler that suggest themselves. One of the wonderful and reassuring things about writing is that, until a work is actually published, nothing is committed beyond retrieval. You can go back and then go back again; and again; until you're satisfied either that you've got it right or, as mostly happens, you've got it about as good as you're ever likely to get it on this dungy earth.

VARIETIES OF FICTION

Much of the above is about plotting narrative fiction in general, only acknowledging through some specific comments that there are actually many differing varieties of fiction; and that in their own characteristic ways, these employ the techniques discussed. The thriller, for example, will by its very nature tend to be strong on plot and often, though not necessarily, on external action; and strong too on impediments to each move that the protagonists attempt to make; and on motivations, like personal survival or the saving of the nation. The love story, on the other hand, is more likely to be concerned with people isolated from public and melodramatic events, with The Great World providing background rather than being, as often with thrillers, part of the subject of the work. Here, for example, is the *Come on* inside cover of A PERFECT BEAST:

"Afraid you're committed to me for life, Jonathan?"

What on earth had made her ask that? That wasn't what she wanted to say to him at all.

He replied angrily, "Cut it out, Rosemary. I'm trying to set the record straight, that's all. I've enjoyed being with you. And I admit my original idea was to ..."

"Get me into bed?" Her body tilted defiantly.

"Right. You've got it," Jonathan said harshly. "But I'm glad you had the sense to stop me the other night, because I've no right to use you ... when I can't give you anything in return."

Rosemary turned her head so that he couldn't see the sudden desolation in her eyes.

"You needn't worry," she lied to him. "Because you don't have anything to give me that I want."

This of course has 'terrible misunderstanding' written all over it, though not too terrible a misunderstanding to be beyond the ingenuity of 190 pages to sort out! Much of this sorting-out action is inner and personal; though Rosemary's school-teaching world does come in as plot source as well as background: (Jonathan is the difficult parent of Rosemary's most intractable pupil — see?)

As well as thriller and love novels, there are works of fantasy, science fiction, Gothic horror, classic detection, social comment, the comic, the autobiographical — all with their own characteristic emphases and tones. The small differences between these varieties of novel, you will need to pick up for yourself through careful reading.

Novels that win literary awards, like the Pulitzer Prize and the Booker and the Miles Franklin, are likely to be more interested in scrutinising human behaviour and exploring the world we inhabit, than in any stark mechanics of plot. But there too, if you look closely, you'll find character realised, and a plot coaxed into existence by one or more of the methods suggested above.

4

Theme

"What the devil does the plot *signify*, except to bring in fine things?"

THE REHEARSAL, George Villiers

T heme, a term out of fashion in literary circles nowadays, refers to what a work is *about* — what a novel might be seen to demonstrate, to signify, to spell out; even to prove. In the words of THE PENGUIN DICTIONARY OF LITERARY TERMS, theme isn't the "subject" of a work, "but rather its central idea which may be stated directly or indirectly". So that when someone remarks of a novel — "I don't know. There's lots of action, the background's interesting, the characters believable enough; but it just doesn't seem to add up to much in the end." — the likelihood is that what this disappointing novel lacks is a strong theme, some unifying central idea or thesis.

TRUE LOVE CONQUERS ALL

One of the most popular themes is: 'true love will find a way.' From the Romance verses of the Middle Ages through Shakespeare's comedies, and eighteenth century drama and letter-novels, Jane Austen's county chronicles, the massive Victorian love stories ... through to the 1994 Pulitzer Prize winner THE SHIPPING NEWS and the whole range of Mills and Boon ... true love does keep finding a way to that final clinch and happy-ever-after. Jack gets his Jill and all's well with the world.

If such a proven and fertile theme is your choice, then the plotting of your novel is, initially, fairly straightforward.

Your lovers keep trying to come together and bond; but something always intervenes, stops them. When they manage to surmount one impediment, another appears; or better, is generated by that very action of surmounting. Then when the next impediment has also been dealt with, there's another again. And so on, until a triumph over a final obstacle/challenge ... reveals sunlit plains extended!

Impediments for your lovers are easy enough to come by. There might already be an existing partner to one of the lovers, as in JANE EYRE. Or some social class incompatibility, as is the case to an extent with PRIDE AND PREJUDICE. It might simply be a lack of cash — a much used problem in novels of some generations back, when before the beloved could be won, the lover had to get some wealth, even if that meant going to America or one of the colonies. Impediments can be existing children; disease; parental authority; an addiction problem; career or study competition; a one-way love; even simple mis-understandings, a frequent device in comedies.

Thomas Hardy even uses malevolent fate as a kind of impediment to the lovers' union, as when in TESS OF THE D'URBERVILLES Tess slips a note beneath Angel Clare's door. But it goes under the carpet so that Angel never gets to know its contents; and Tess is thereby switched to a road that leads to an act of murder and to her hanging for it. This of course is a variant of the true love theme, in that the novel doesn't end in the lovers' union and happiness. Angel and Tess do come together for a week, though, before her death.

A reversal of the theme 'True love will find a way' would be 'All for love and the world well lost.' Here, the lovers choose between their love for each other, and their very lives. ANTONY AND CLEOPATRA and ROMEO AND JULIET can readily be played to fetch out this theme; and the WUTHERING HEIGHTS theme 'Love rejected, love betrayed, generates violence and destruction' is another kind of reversal.

Shakespeare, in several of his romantic comedies, devised a fascinating way of dealing with this situation of getting lovers past impediments. His heroines disguise themselves as males; and this enables them then to intervene in the flow of hostile events that threaten to divide the lovers, and to redirect these hostile events in a happier direction. Then at the appropriate moment, this intelligent and capable heroine doffs her disguise and claims her lover and, as the Fool Feste sings to a group in TWELFTH NIGHT, "Journeys end in lovers meeting."

There are love stories today where the heroine not so much disguises herself but takes herself behind the scenes, probably unknown to the other characters, and somehow deals with the impediment(s) whilst out of sight there.

Here are some further themes:

➤ Courage will conquer: Alan Marshall's I CAN JUMP PUDDLES.

➤ Crime does not *(or does!)* pay: About a million titles spell this out!

➤ Love heals wounds: Annie Proulx's THE SHIPPING NEWS.

➤ A good woman can save a bad man: Ugh! But Victorians loved it!

➤ Jealousy destroys: OTHELLO.

➤ You can lose your life trying too hard to protect it: Virginia Woolf looks at this in MRS DALLOWAY.

➤ Motherhood is sacred: American denominational magazines love this theme.

➤ I could be bound within a nutshell and count myself king of infinite space: That's HAMLET. "Bliss" perhaps?

➤ Now get you to my lady's chamber, and tell her, let her paint an inch thick, to this favour must she come: HAMLET again, cupping a human skull in his hands!

➤ There is a providence that shapes our ends, rough hew them how we will: HAMLET is virtually a Theme Seeker's Manual! The religious, the fatalists, and those believing in astrology, could build novels around this theme.

➤ It's all lies; but lies sometimes direct towards the truth: JOHNNO. And the passage in which that, occurs:

> "It's all lies," Johnno would say. And in the end, perhaps, it is. Johnno's false disguise is the one image of him that lasted, and the only one that could have jumped out from the page and demanded of me these few hours of my

*attention. Maybe, in the end, even the lies we tell define us.
And better, some of them, than our most earnest attempts
at the truth.*

The situation that catches up this thematic preoccupation occurs in the novel's first episode when the narrator, Dante, going through his dead father's effects, comes across an old school photo in which the prankster Johnno appears "in false disguise". The rest of the novel is an exploration of this territory — what *is* true about a person?

Most sayings, axioms, proverbs, even platitudes, will yield a basic theme; though you would be aiming to have your treatment of that axiom/proverb rather more sophisticated than its initial and platitudinous form.

To have a strong theme in mind enables you to select events and characters most suitable for such a theme, and for its expression. It will also help you decide your novel's conclusion, which obviously must be the outcome predicated by your particular theme.

Sometimes, however, you get first in mind your major characters and your plot, so that in a sense you have then to distil a theme or themes from these. What truth will give coherence to this plot? What values and insights will underwrite and give significance to your characters' actions?

CHILD INTO MAN

So if you were to choose as your theme, 'To grow up is to confront both challenge, and loss,' then you would be thinking around a central character facing situations that are impelling him/her into adulthood. Probably you'd have that character keep recoiling and retreating from the changes and demands that go with growing up; until an ultimate challenge when, if your novel is to have an upbeat ending, your character would accept maturity, accommodate the changes. There you have the 'Boy into man' theme or its feminine equivalent — that is, a *rites of passage* into adulthood.

The above is of course something of the theme and structure of THE CATCHER IN THE RYE. Check through each of Holden's incidents, see how many of them are in effect challenges to him, and how many of them he runs from. It's no wonder Holden has this recurring concern about those ducks in Central Park ponds, where *they* escape to each year, from the change and challenge of Winter.

> "Hey listen", I said. "By any chance, do you happen to know where they go, the ducks, when it gets all frozen over? Do you happen to know, by any chance?"

The place where Holden does feel unthreatened, though, is the Natural History Museum, where there was never change. The Eskimo figure would still be standing immobile, fishing; the stuffed birds always winging south; the same deer by the same pond. "Certain things should stay the way they are ... " Holden laments when reflecting on this. "I know that's impossible, but it's too bad anyway."

Gradually, though, on his odyssey around New York, Holden comes to acknowledge that he must in fact move through change and into adulthood. This realisation, and its acceptance, comes to a considerable extent through his sister Phoebe.

First, he finds highly offensive graffiti on her school wall; and then, seemingly, everywhere; even in the Egyptian tomb in the Museum. He reflects wryly that even when he dies, and they stick him in a cemetery with a tombstone stating his name and dates of birth and death — under that, he's positive, someone will add "---- you!" So it is borne in on him that he simply cannot protect Phoebe from all the brutal, ugly ill-will thus directed in this world against innocence and good will.

Then in the penultimate scene of the novel, when he is watching Phoebe riding the carousel horses, he realises that though in reaching out for the gold ring she is quite likely to fall, there is nothing he can do about that either; nor indeed should he try to do anything.

> "The thing with kids is, if they want to grab for the gold ring, you have to let them do it, and not say anything. If they fall off, they fall off."

If Phoebe is to grow and flower — well, hazards are inescapably part of the package. The only alternative is the undeveloped, unfulfilled life of the boy/man, girl/woman. And presumably Holden transfers something of this insight to himself, because he too, uncertain and bruised, reaches at last for the gold ring of responsible adulthood. At least that's how many read the sudden rain that comes at this precise point. All the parents scatter for shelter; but Holden elects to sit it out, letting it stream over him, soaking him. A benedictory, baptismal rain? A blessing on his decision?

SECONDARY THEMES

Themes can additionally be used to counterpoint other themes, in something of the same way that sub-plots can reinforce or qualify a main plot. The primary theme in WUTHERING HEIGHTS, for instance: 'Love thwarted breeds violence and self-destruction', might be seen as dooming the Heathcliff and Catherine love from its very beginning, given the environment of conflict and brutality into which it was born and in which it had to exist. No other ending to such a love story seems possible — if you accept the 'Love thwarted ..' as the theme. But the love between Hareton and the second Catherine is born into a similarly hostile and brutal world — The Heights of Heathcliff and Joseph. Their love, however, does prosper. Is it true, then, that Heathcliff and Catherine really were doomed from the start? Perhaps the theme should be restated as: 'Love thwarted *by betrayal* ... '? So the Hareton and second Catherine love story actually provides a kind of audit of the earlier love story; and in the event, perhaps, a thumbs down? The Heathcliff and Catherine love didn't have to end tragically. Catherine's betrayal of her love, and Heathcliff's perversion of it, are what made it do so?

The theme of the Hareton and Catherine sub-plot, then, acts to counterpoint the theme of the Heathcliff and Catherine main plot; and the effect of this is to leave us not with predigested conclusions about the nature and realities of love relationships, but with a lot of thinking to do and questions to ask.

The very bits-of-business in each of these two co-existing love stories invite us to compare them. The characters' names are either identical or similar — two Catherines, and the echoic Heathcliff and Hareton. Each Catherine had a choice between two males — Cathy 1, between Heathcliff and Edgar; Cathy 2, between Hareton and the sickly Linton. (The first though, chose the wrong male, while the latter, after having had the wrong one forced on her, chose the right one: a significant difference?) Each male suffered brutality from a more powerful male — Heathcliff from Hindley, Hareton from Heathcliff. Further, each brutal male suffered in turn the loss of a beloved female — Hindley of Frances, Heathcliff of his Catherine. Indeed, and strangely perhaps, each central male is linked by name to the natural world as no other character in the novel is — heath and cliff, and hare(bell). Plot and sub-plot do indeed interact then, very much; and the significance of this interaction has considerable implications for theme.

Not all readers will agree with the account of WUTHERING HEIGHTS outlined above. This is no doubt because we all respond to quality fiction much as we do to the events of 'real life', fetching to each our own particular nature, our individual experiences and our adopted values. But whatever you decide finally about the themes this novel embodies, you can hardly avoid taking into account this juxtaposing of main plot and sub-plot, and the way each one seems to throw into question the very 'meaning' of the other.

MULTIPLE THEMES

Themes do not always act to challenge or destabilise one the other, though. They can do the direct opposite, reinforce each other. There is something of this happening in HENRY IV, PT I, discussed earlier. You will recall that the play has three settings — court, battlefield, and tavern. In each, you have violent predators. The King has seized the throne in a coup; the battlefield rebels want to seize the kingdom for themselves; and down in the tavern, commoners seize purses on the highway. The theme? In every walk of life — the bushrangers operate! All three plots announce it! Straddling these three settings, though, and moving easily and naturally between them, is Prince Hal (who is not a bushranger); learning about all the sorts and conditions of predators plaguing the kingdom he is eventually, as Henry V, to inherit. There's theme in that too! Shakespeare provides three different tones, by the way, for his three settings and three sub-plots. The low life area is comic; the court is person-intense, close up; the battlefield is public, big screen action.

HAPPINESS THEMES

Katherine Mansfield's short story "Bliss" makes an interesting study because its theme is rather elusive. The title directs us to it; but the problem for the reader is to decide quite what the story is saying about bliss in relation to the main character, Bertha.

Bertha's bliss is depicted in various ways, chiefly sensuous. It's a kind of exquisite consciousness of being alive and being happy, of delighting in everything, every sensation:

> *...as though you'd suddenly swallowed a bright piece of that late afternoon sun and it burned in your bosom, sending out a little shower of sparks into every particle, into every finger and toe ...*

But for Bertha, there's a problem in expressing this bliss, a problem of social constraints explored through the questioning:

> *Why be given a body if you have to keep it shut up in a case like a rare, rare fiddle?*

There's also a problem constraining Bertha's relationship with Little B, and that problem is Nanny.

> *How absurd it was. Why have a baby if it has to be kept — not in a case like a rare, rare fiddle — but in another woman's arms?*

This questioning technique is the author's mode of signalling some as yet unspecified danger for Bertha and her happiness. There is a feeling of impending change; and while the reader moves with Bertha through her sense of identification with the exquisite, flowering pear tree which seems to encapsulate her feeling of having reached some peak of happiness, a sabotaging undercurrent of projected and threatening change is constantly present. Ironically, too, as the reader becomes uneasily aware, the pear tree is also an image of Bertha's "woman find", the enigmatic Pearl Fulton to whom Bertha feels so close. And it is Pearl Fulton who in fact takes Bertha's happiness away, because she takes Harry. Harry, as well as Little B, is "in another woman's arms".

Before this realisation, Bertha is led, through her evening and likewise through a deepening of her sensation of bliss, into a sharing with Pearl Fulton, within a circle of moonlight, of the beauty and perfection of the flowering pear tree; led to a point, for the first time in her life, of desire for her husband. Now she desires him:

> *...ardently! ardently! The word ached in her ardent body!*
> *Was this what that feeling of bliss had been leading up to?*
> *But then —*

The reader doesn't know what qualification Bertha was proposing because, soon after, Bertha sees Harry and Miss Fulton together; and her 'bliss' is shattered.

So what theme or themes emerge from these events?

There's a sense in which the story says: 'Happiness is a fragile thing. Treasure it, it might not last.' Shakespeare's TWELFTH NIGHT can be seen as proclaiming just this too. "Present mirth hath present laughter. Youth's a stuff will not endure." And although that play finishes with all the lovers finding beloveds — though not at all the beloveds they'd been expecting! — the final scene is not betrothal and celebration, but an empty stage with a world-weary, cynical, professional Fool singing, bleakly, of the wind and the rain, "For the rain — it raineth *every day*."

This theme, of the fragility of happiness, is suggested in Mansfield's story by the way that Bertha's bliss is linked to the pear tree in full flower, with the notion that such efflorescence is part of the natural cycle. Full flowering is reached; then, inevitably, fallen away from. There is a point at which Bertha comes to something of an awareness of this: "I'm too happy — too happy!" she murmurs, and it is here that she seems to see "the lovely pear tree with its wide open blossoms as a symbol of her own life".

HAPPINESS BUILT ON ILLUSION

There's at least one other theme, and perhaps a more important one, running through this story. It's an ironic, satiric theme, and a painful one; of happiness often being built on an illusion. The story could come into that category Thomas Hardy termed "Satires of Circumstance", stories and events in which some kind of circumstance renders human happiness illusory because it's based on false premises, on misreadings of the way things actually are. Certainly Bertha, on this reading, would seem to have done nothing directly to precipitate the crushing 'circumstance' in which she finds herself. So the satire is of human beings as 'Life's play-things'!

Almost surely, though, the reader would have an uneasy suspicion that Bertha has in fact played some part in her own downfall. There's that rather odd sentence when, at the dinner party, they were all waiting for Miss Fulton:

> *Came another tiny moment, while they waited, laughing and talking, just a trifle too much at their ease, a trifle too unaware.*

Unaware of what?

Perhaps all those waiting at that precise point, except Harry, who is in a different category, are being satirised for smugness, for choosing to live as a precious, affected little group: modern, thrilling friends, writers and painters and poets or people keen on social questions? Think of "Mug" with his monocle. "Face" with her coat and the monkeys. Eddie Warren the poet with his "fears" of his taxi driver, and his exaggerated speech.

Is it because Bertha is really living at this distance from reality (think of how she creates the fruit, an image of how she constructs her life perhaps?) that everything she touches is at a remove from her; even her husband? Is this why, even at the end of the story when she knows the truth about Harry and Miss Fulton, when she runs over to the long windows and cries: "Oh, what is going to happen now?" — is this why the final line of the story reads:

> *But the pear tree was as lovely as ever and as full of flower and as still?*

Do we read this line as suggesting, perhaps, that the pear tree is in fact removed from Bertha, and involved in real life and the natural cycle, in a way that Bertha herself is not? Perhaps the pear tree symbolises happiness, which Miss Fulton in a sense has taken away from Bertha and made hers; so the pear tree hasn't itself changed? And could this final line be. suggesting that Bertha's life has not altered? All that has changed is her perception of it; her unawareness has simply become awareness.

One of the most ironic lines in the story must occur when Bertha is farewelling her guests and we are told that she felt, "this self of hers was taking leave of her forever". She was, of course, feeling completely changed because she was filled with this newborn desire for her husband; and in the story's context this is ironic indeed, in that it represents a step at last towards moving out of her unaware world. But as it stands, it is a very sad line. It turns out to be true in a way that Bertha did not remotely foresee.

Well, what do these readings suggest by way of theme? Perhaps:

➤ Not to involve oneself with the real world, can be self-destructive?

➤ One can't live in a bubble, because bubbles burst?

➤ Once something's lost, it's lost forever?

All of these have some plausibility, And yet — not quite right?

So what about: 'Ignorance is bliss?' This would give a rather awful irony to the story's title. Is it only ignorance of what life is really like, that allows bliss to be experienced? This would be a disillusioned, downbeat ending to the happiness theme.

PLOTS AND THEMES TOGETHER

Finally, for this chapter, let's take an example of plot and sub-plot and theme(s) ... all working together in most of the ways outlined above.

Shakespeare's MEASURE FOR MEASURE is a close, hard look at human sexual behaviour. The main plot concerns the sexually extremely repressive Lord Angelo, who is left in charge of the State while the Duke, sickened by the lechery throughout his city but unwilling to confront it, leaves for a time. Angelo promptly shuts down the brothels and enforces the city's harsh laws.

First ensnared by this clampdown is a young noble, Claudio. He is sentenced to execution for getting his betrothed with child. Isabella, a young nun who is Claudio's sister, pleads with Angelo for her brother's life; whereupon the saintly Angelo lusts so mightily after her that he offers to reverse that death sentence if she herself will fornicate with him!

Throughout all this, the reps of the city's brothels — Pompey the pimp and Mistress Overdone the madam — strive in full comic mode to convince the authorities that unless they geld all the males in the city, they can forget about No-No sex laws. That is, whatever one might feel about sexual licence, savage sexual repression is not likely to prove a very productive response. Not even, perhaps, when such 'repression' takes the seemingly positive form of endowing chastity with highest value? Isabella-the-chaste decides to reject Angelo's offer — that is, to allow her brother to die rather than lose her precious virginity in saving him. "More than our brother, is our chastity!" she exclaims. But is this 'value' really to be preferred to Angelo's rape-per-blackmail? Sexual chastity above even *life itself?*

Anyway, both main plot and comic sub-plot spell out these considerations, as does indeed the very minor sub-plot of Lucio the nobleman-lecher. The whole sorry business is sorted out when the absent Duke returns; in fact he hadn't actually been away, but watching all from the wings!

This part of the play isn't particularly convincing, and one might suspect that Shakespeare couldn't think of any really satisfactory way to end what he'd started, consistent with his theme(s). Angelo and Claudio each gets forgiven, plus a wife; and the Duke, for reasons not entirely clear, gets Isabella, who by now has had her priorities more humanely ordered. Lucio, whose sole "sin" is general and fairly cheerful promiscuity, gets the only punishment meted out. He is made to marry a whore! All this makes rather for some thematic muddle, though 'Judge not that ye be not judged' survives clearly enough. This uncertainty with theme would explain why MEASURE FOR MEASURE has been labelled a 'problem play'. Plotting and themes get themselves out of sync. It can happen even with La Creme!

Considerations of theme are still, at time of writing, up and working. Here is a part of director Richard Buckham's Sydney interview with playwright (of AUTUMN) Terence Crawford:

> RB. *If writing is intuitive for you, how do you deal with the big questions of theme for example? Do you know, for example, what you want the audience to leave the theatre with?*
>
> TC. *Very generally, I think that all works of art have three messages. The world is a terrible place, the world is a wonderful place, or the world is a difficult place. The last of those, it seems to me, is the realm of mature art. A cheap comedy is one that conveys the first message, a cheap tragedy conveys the second. But a rich comedy is one where the world is a wonderful place but also*

difficult, and a rich tragedy has a world that is terrible and difficult. Then there are plays where the world is just difficult! Looking at something rich like Shakespeare's late romances, for example, you get the sense of the world becoming a more and more difficult place to negotiate. I've no interest in stating the first two messages. So I guess I always opt for the other. The world is difficult, even when it is wonderful or terrible, and all we can do is look after one another.

You'd go a long way to find a wiser statement on theme than Terence Crawford's.

5

Beginnings & Endings

Homerus auditorem in media res rapit.
Homer precipitates his readers into the midst of the action.

HORACE (loosely translated)

I f the opening of your novel doesn't highjack your reader, you'll likely not have any reader; and if your concluding pages don't satisfy that reader, then nobody much is going to be killing for your next book!

It has been suggested that the best way to begin a piece of fiction is with an earthquake; then work up to a climax! This is of course a mite extravagant: most of us would have difficulty working out where to go on to, from such an already climactic opening. But the point being made is a sound one. Begin with something that will capture your reader.

This, for the most part, resolves to a simple begin-with-action; not necessarily explosive action, as the earthquake above; or an aircraft crash or an assassination or a bar room brawl. Even physical action can be less violent than this. Gerald hands in his resignation. Brooke tells Merlie that their relationship is ended. Brennan persuades Kylie to sleep with him; or to open a craft shop in a country town; or to have his child. Alice sets off to visit her grandfather. Holden Caulfield runs away from school.

Of course, a great deal of action need not be physical at all; or even external. There is inner action — emotional and mental; feeling and thinking. There is character action, in which two or more characters strike sparks off one another, as with the Hotspur and Glendower exchange in Chapter 2. There is even a kind of action associated with setting — the implications of particular location, backdrop; tensions arising from these. Hardy's description of Egdon Heath, opening THE RETURN OF THE NATIVE, and the first paragraphs of E.M. Forster's A PASSAGE TO INDIA, are instances of these latter.

PHYSICAL-ACTION OPENING

Here is an example combining several kinds of action:

"Tom Fobble's Day!"

The first snowball caught William in the teeth. The second burst on his forehead; the third on his balaclava helmet.

He let go of his sledge, and ran, blindly. The snowballs kept hitting him, on the back, on the legs, softly, quietly, but he couldn't stand them.

The snow gathered between the iron of his clogs and the curved wood of the sole and built into rockers of ice. His ankles twisted and he fell over, trying not to cry. He curled himself against the attack.

But it had stopped. He opened his eyes. He wasn't even out of range. Stewart Allman had stopped throwing and was sitting on William's sledge.

William stood up. "Give us me sledge!" It had taken him a day and a morning to build it out of an old crate.

"It isn't yours," said Stewart Allman.

"It is!"

"It isn't. I've Tom Fobbled it."

"You can't! You can't Tom Fobble sledges! Only marbles!"

"What are you going to do about it?" said Stewart Allman.

Alan Garner writes sophisticated and often disturbing fiction for children and adolescents, and the above is TOM FOBBLE'S DAY. First, almost straight action, the snowball assault. Then, character clash. And finally, an announcement of the novel's preoccupation, theme — which promises quite a deal of action ahead as the novel traces what William is "going to do about it". One would hardly expect to see the odious Stewart Allman emerge finally triumphant?

Victor Kelleher is another successful writer for young people (and adults). Here is the opening of his THE MASTER OF THE GROVE. While there is hardly any physical movement in it — an anonymous, supine boy and a static landscape — there is an awareness of considerable prior action, which must flow into future action because the boy has to deal with both what has happened and what this will demand of him.

> When he opened his eyes he could remember nothing, not even his own name. It was almost like waking up for the very first time, looking out through bewildered eyes upon a world he did not understand. Everything about the past — his own identity, where he had come from — was a total blank. He knew only that he was extremely cold and that his head ached unbearably. Groaning softly to himself, he rolled over and looked about him. It took him a moment or two to focus clearly; then he found that he was somewhere in a wood, lying stretched out near the edge of a deep bank of snow. There was no trace of colour in the scene before him: overhead, the sky was a dull, wintry grey; and the wood itself was etched starkly in black and white, the dark trunks of trees rising up out of a uniform blanket of snow.

This opening probably draws something of its force from its archetypal character. That is, our very first experience as a human being is to discover ourselves dumped into a strange and hostile world, with seemingly only our own resources to draw on for our survival. As King Lear recognised: "We came crying hither: Thou know'st the first time that we smell the air, we waul and cry."

This, too, is probably why Daniel Defoe's ROBINSON CRUSOE endures; being born and being castaway, are situations we deep-down recognise and respond to. As, indeed, we respond to challenges to our territory; which is the basic situation the Alan Garner opening is tapping.

DESCRIPTIVE OPENINGS

Here is part of the beginning of Charles Dickens' BLEAK HOUSE:

Fog everywhere. Fog up the river, where it flows among green aits and meadows; fog down the river where it rolls defiled among the tiers of shipping, and the waterside pollutions of a great (and dirty) city. Fog on the Essex marshes, fog on the Kentish heights. Fog creeping into the cabooses of collier-brigs, fog lying out on the yards, and hovering in the rigging of great ships; fog drooping on the gunwales of barges and small boats. Fog in the eyes and throats of ancient Greenwich pensioners, wheezing by the firesides of their wards; fog in the stem and bowl of the afternoon pipe of the wrathful skipper, down in his close cabin; fog cruelly pinching the toes and fingers of his shivering little 'prentice boy on deck. Chance people on the bridges peeping over the parapets into a nether sky of fog, with fog all round them, as if they were up in a balloon, and hanging in misty clouds.

Gas looming through the fog in divers places in the streets, much as the sun may, from the spongy fields, be seen to loom by husbandman and ploughboy. Most of the shops lighted two hours before their time — as the gas seems to know, for it has a haggard and unwilling look.

The raw afternoon is rawest, and the dense fog is densest, and the muddy streets are muddiest, near that leaden-headed old corporation: Temple Bar. And hard by Temple Bar, in Lincoln's Inn Hall, at the very heart of the fog, sits the Lord High Chancellor in his High Court of Chancery.

This is a straight and vivid description of London fog in Victorian times. But it is also strongly thematic, in that the fog acts as image for the British justice system in those days, at the Temple and Lincoln's Inn. According to Dickens-the-reformer, the Law too was fog-like, impenetrable. And right at the heart of British Law, as at the heart of the blinding fog — the High Court of Chancery, where wills were contested and inheritances decided. There, all was so dense and baffling that contestants could win a large legacy, yet be ruined by the costs of doing so.

It is an appropriate opening for BLEAK HOUSE, because almost every character in the novel is in some way groping around a Chancery suit, or connected destructively with someone else who is.

FOREBODING OPENINGS

Almost equally well known is the opening to Ford Maddox Ford's THE GOOD SOLDIER.

> This is the saddest story I have ever heard. We had known the Ashburnhams for nine seasons of the town of Nauheim with an extreme intimacy — or, rather with an acquaintanceship as loose and easy and yet as close as a good glove's with your hand. My wife and I knew Captain Ashburnham as well as it was possible to know anybody, and yet, in another sense, we knew nothing at all about them. This is, I believe, a state of things only possible with English people of whom, till today, when I sit down to puzzle out what I know of this sad affair, I knew nothing whatever. Six months ago I had never been to England, and, certainly, I had never sounded the depths of an English heart. I had known the shallows.

Such an opening is full of that kind of prefiguring termed 'forebodings'. An overall sadness is adumbrated twice. There is quite an element of puzzle, too, which narrator and reader are set up to pursue together. Most of all, there is this suggestion that one can know another person so well ... and yet not know this person at all. This is certainly the basis of the novel's story. As a theme, it is by no means new. Oscar Wilde used something similar in THE PICTURE OF DORIAN GREY and so did R.L. Stevenson in DR JEKYLL AND MR HYDE. Ford's work, though, is perhaps the more complex and sophisticated in technique.

ARRESTING OPENINGS

Here is quite an arresting opening:

> I keep thinking that I have a tunnel in my chest. The path the bullet took, burrowing through the flesh and sinew and whatever muscle the bullet encountered (I am not the macho-muscled type, not at five eleven and one hundred

eighteen pounds). Anyway, the bullet went through my chest and out again. The wound has healed and there is no pain. The two ends of the tunnel are closed although there's a puckering of the skin at both ends of the tunnel. And a faint redness. The puckering has a distinct design, like the old vaccination scar on my father's arm. Years from now, the wound will probably hurt the way my father's old war wounds hurt him, the wounds he received in those World War Two battles. My mother always jokes about the wounds: oh, not the wounds themselves but the fact that he professes to forecast weather by the phantom pains and throbbings in his arms and legs.

Will my wound ache like his when I am his age?

And will I be able to tell when the rain will fall by the pain whistling through the tunnel in my chest?

This could probably impress as an action opening — wounds and bullets and battles. Actually, of course, there is not the slightest physical movement throughout, nor for that matter is there any physical setting. All you have are thoughts, reflections; and anonymous ones at that. The passage, though, is heavy with prior action — prior violent action; and it very soon gets to project violent action ahead. Additionally, this introduction presents character; a young man (we realise he is this from his attitude to his father and mother, I think?) who in an aloof, almost wry manner meditates on a wound made by a bullet that ploughed a tunnel right through his chest. Robert Cormier, American writer of thrillers for 'young adults', certainly manages in AFTER THE FIRST DEATH to get the reader in!

CHARACTER OPENINGS

ONCE WERE WARRIORS opens with fierce characterisation, and an intolerable situation presented. The reader knows, within a dozen lines, that this character and this situation cannot but emerge into boil-over.

Bastard, she'd think, looking out her back kitchen window. Lucky white bastard, at that glimpse of two-storey house through its surround of big old trees and its oh so secure greater surround of rolling green pastureland, while she —

Clicking her tongue, Oh to hell with him. Or good luck to him, if she wasn't in too bad a mood.

Good luck to you, white man, for being born into your sweet world, and bad luck to you, Beth Heke (who used to be a Ransfield but not that life was so much better then), for being married to an arsehole. And yet I love him. I just can't help myself, I love the black, fist-happy bastard. And she'd light another smoke ...

OPENING TO A LOVE STORY

As good an opening to a piece of fiction as you'd find, and one that uses many kinds of action, is that of Shakespeare's ANTONY AND CLEOPATRA. This play explores many issues and themes; but its main interest must surely be the love story.

What you have, is an older man of heroic, generous but rash temperament, at the peak of his political and military reputation. He falls — plunges — for the dusky, not-quite-so-young Queen of Egypt, who is worldly wise, politically astute, blazingly sexual and whose throne is being threatened by Rome. Is it love they feel for each other? Or is it, on Antony's part, simply a mighty sexual infatuation? And on Cleopatra's something of that too; but even more, political scheming to defend her kingdom?

The pressures mount on their relationship to the point where they have to decide whether, for each, life without the other would be intolerable. Hence, death preferable.

Here's a brief account of the opening of the play:

Two Roman soldiers enter, gossiping about their great general's notorious affair. They see it as simply "dotage". Antony's eyes, they say, which used to survey great battlefields, "now bend, now turn, upon a tawny front." Their great leader of armies has become "a strumpet's fool", merely "the bellows and the fan to cool a gypsy's lust".

This view reflects the strict Roman ideal, in which public duty and self-discipline are the proclaimed virtues. With his own nation, Antony's behaviour can provoke only scorn and disgust.

But must we accept this Roman judgement of Mark Antony? How genuine is this mighty Roman's love?

Shakespeare immediately proffers us the opportunity to check out the couple for ourselves.

"Look where they come ... Behold and see."

Enter Antony and Cleopatra. And Cleopatra instantly takes up our very question. To Antony:

"If this be love indeed, tell me — how MUCH?"

That is, is your professed love greater than your attachment to your Roman values? Roman honour? Because, the astute Cleopatra realises, it is with these that she competes.

Antony's reply?

"There's beggary in the love that can be reckon'd."

That is, again, it's a beggarly, poverty-stricken sort of love if it can be quantified by a 'How much?' In Antony's proclaimed scale of values, love should be without limit.

Cleopatra sees through this romantic extravagance to the hard reality that if Antony is to retain his position astride the whole Mediterranean world, his declared love for her will have to be forfeited. She replies, confrontingly:

"I'll set a bourne (boundary) how far to be belov'd."

"Then must thou needs find out NEW heaven, NEW earth!"

This universe, Antony is boasting, simply isn't big enough to contain his love!

So in the first few minutes of the play, we have three positions staked out. Rome's first: Antony's love is unRoman and contemptible. Then Antony's: his love is boundless. Then Cleopatra's: Antony's love is only too likely to prove very bounded indeed. It's Cleopatra or Rome. Never both!

But, "Let Rome in Tiber melt!" Antony declaims. "And the wide arch of the Empire fall!" Enormities for any Roman to utter; but from that particular monumental Roman of his time ... ! Which the more realistic Cleopatra well understands.

"Excellent ... FALSEHOOD!" she decides.

The rest of the play comprises a series of testings of each of those three positions. Will Antony's love survive Cleopatra's betrayal when, with her fleet, she flees from battle? Will it survive his bitter realisation that the closest and most trusted of his soldier-comrades are turning their backs on him because of Cleopatra, crossing over to Caesar's forces? Will their love survive

Antony's abandonment of her and his return to the Roman fold? Or Cleopatra's attempts to do a tricky deal with Rome? Or Antony's political marriage to Caesar's sister?

The love between the two does, in fact — astonishingly, miraculously — triumph over all this. For each one, nothing is of more importance finally than the other. Antony, mistakenly believing Cleopatra dead, takes his own life; and Cleopatra, learning of this and rejecting life without him, retires with her maids Iras and Charmian and does likewise.

> Give me my robe, put on my crown, I have
> Immortal longings in me. Now no more
> The juice of Egypt's grape shall moist this lip.
> Yare, yare, good Iras; quick. Methinks I hear
> Antony call: I see him rouse himself
> To praise my noble act. I hear him mock
> The luck of Caesar ... Husband, I come:
> Now to that name, my courage prove my title!
> I am fire, and air; my other elements
> I give to baser life. So, have you done?
> Come then, and take the last warmth from my lips.
> Farewell, kind Charmian, Iras, long farewell.
> The stroke of death is as a lover's pinch,
> Which hurts, and is desired ...

All this, the whole five long acts, is skilfully laid out, and set in motion, over those first few dozen lines of the play. So it's some beginning!

ENDINGS

Endings are to an extent beginnings in reverse. Whatever issue, dilemma, question, problem, thematic statement, your first pages set forth, becomes specifically resolved, answered, rounded off, in your last. The lovers clinch. The villain is unmasked. The hero/heroine is either rescued, or perishes. The US cavalry (or marines, these days) thunders (or helicopters) to the rescue. The Elf King confounds the Black Magician and is restored to the throne of Moggyddyn. The extent and status of Antony and Cleopatra's love is affirmed forever. Beth Heke returns, grown in wisdom and spirit, to her people.

In Mark Twain's PUDD'NHEAD WILSON, set in the pre-Civil War South of the United States, the illegitimate, thirty-one-parts-white/one-part-black child of the slave nursemaid, Roxy, is switched by his mother at eight months old with the rich white child, Tom, whom he resembles. He is switched by his mother, not because she doesn't love him but because she does, so that he might never be "sold down the river" as a slave. Ironically, finally, that is what turns out to be his fate.

As the novel concludes, the false one-part-black "Tom", now an adult, is sentenced to life for murder. However, with the truth about the "switch" having come out, he is pardoned on an appeal by the creditors of the murdered man. They claim that, as a slave, "Tom" is in fact their "property". Twain, in a very famous turn-the-opening-upside-down ending, concludes with savage (and economical) irony:

> Everybody saw that there was reason in this. Everybody granted that if "Tom" were white and free it would be unquestionably right to punish him — it would be no loss to anybody; but to shut up a valuable slave for life — that was quite another matter.

> As soon as the Governor understood the case, he pardoned Tom at once, and the creditors sold him down the river.

These above are closed endings, the most frequent kind. A novel can finish open-ended though; that is, with the sequence of events broken off, but their significance or their sequelae left unstated, uncertain. It has been suggested that WUTHERING HEIGHTS is one such, because you can read the final lines as setting forth either reunion in death for Heathcliff and Catherine, or obliteration for them, following love betrayed during life. The ending of CATCHER is also ambivalent, with Holden finally in some sort of institution; although immediately before, he'd seemed to have completed satisfactorily the transition from adolescence to adulthood. Each of these endings has the effect of throwing us back to a reassessment of its particular novel as a whole; especially back to their respective openings, to see what was actually being signalled there. This makes for compelling fiction. But such an open ending to a novel should be appropriate to the issues and themes raised in it, and should be seen to have flowed, when one looks back, from all that is in the novel. It should not be simply the result of an author not knowing how to bring his/her novel to a conclusion!

It is awkward to give examples of endings, because mostly the process of unravelling mysteries, of lovers explaining to each other their misunderstandings and misjudgments, extend across many pages or whole chapters. But here is one where enough can be quoted to exemplify the points above. It is from Jessica Anderson's TIRRA LIRRA BY THE RIVER, an elegant and moving journey-into-the-past novel. It concludes with recollection of an incident that had somewhat troubled, even haunted, Nora Porteus throughout her life; a funeral, with an accompanying black dress being pulled over her head:

> I am almost angry that there continues to flash on my memory that old chimera, the step of a horse, the nod of a plume, and that always, always, it is accompanied for a second by a choking chaos of grief. But one evening, when I have sat too long under the mango tree, and I turn my head and see the first whiff of darkness extend along the grass and deepen the pockets of foliage, I remember a black cloth. A black dress, dropped over my head from above. It passes over my aching eyes, my swollen mouth, and is arranged on my shoulders by someone whose waist is at a level with my eyes. I stare at the buckle of her belt, mother-of-pearl, until it dissolves in wetness and flashes with long stars, pink and sea-green stars. The same wetness diffuses the darkening grass of Grace's garden, and then out of a moment of groping, of intense confusion, comes the step of a horse, the nod of a plume, come the plumed heads of the curbed horses at my father's funeral.
>
> Later, I remember that there was a voice, too, with rolling rs.
>
> "A fine ceremony, madam! A verrry fine ceremony!"
>
> I think it consoled me, a little. I think ceremony always has, a little.

Finally, to bring together beginnings and endings — two pairs of each. The first is from Tom Keneally's BRING LARKS AND HEROES. We are introduced to Corporal Phelim Halloran, per character sketch; and the setting of the early colony in New South Wales is established.

> At the world's worse end, it is Sunday afternoon in
> February. Through the edge of the forest a soldier moves
> without any idea that he's caught in a mesh of sunlight
> and shade. Corporal Halloran's this fellow's name. He's a
> lean boy taking long strides through the Sabbath heat.
> Visibly, he has the illusion of knowing where he's going ...

An alert reader might pick up here that this character "moves without any idea that he's caught in a mesh of sunlight and shade" and that "he had the illusion of knowing where he's going". These are indeed the situations of fate-hounded Corporal Halloran, whose experiences encompass the love of his "secret bride" Ann Rush and, finally, hanging. Here is part of the conclusion:

> The hanging man was back. He had the hairy noose over
> Halloran's head and tightened and arranged it with small
> tugs that could afford to be kindly.
>
> "Good-bye," he said simply. He was a stupid man, full of
> drama and business.
>
> Halloran squinted out at the brown scars of faces,
> luminously agog, aimed at him.
>
> Snarl of drums. The Government House party arrived, His
> Excellency forebearing, with his right hand, to address the
> crowd.
>
> The Provost-Marshal's sword rose and fell. The
> waggon-teams began pulling. He had to dance slowly as
> the waggon floor began to move without him. He could
> actually hear the cheering ...

The final example comes from Shirley Hazzard's THE BAY OF NOON. This opening details physical action — an aircraft crash; but notice that the force of the passage is strongly thematic. The beginning and ending of TRANSIT OF VENUS, probably this powerful author's best known novel, are rather similar.

> A military plane crashed that winter on Mount Vesuvius.
> The plane had taken off from Naples in a fog; some hours
> afterwards it was reported missing. The search went on for
> hundreds of miles around — over the Ionian Sea, and at
> Catania, at Catanzaro. Two days later, when the fog lifted,

we could see the wreck quite clearly, crumbled against the snow-streaked cone of the volcano, overlooking the airfield from which it had set out. No one had thought of looking close to home.

Theme is caught up again in the final paragraphs; indeed, these paragraphs compose little more than reflection on theme.

The engine subsiding, we re-enter the elements. It is dark ...

The outcome of such a crossing is immaterial. ... Equipped to search, we justify ourselves by ranging as far afield as possible, in order to render a plausible account, to be able to say, "I looked everywhere". But it is not by such journeys as these that one approaches home. ... We are like those early explorers of Australia who died of thirst on expeditions to the dead centre of a continent, always thinking they must come ultimately to water — to an inland sea, to a lake, a river, a cascade. Deceived by salt deposits, by rivers that flow inland, by the fossils of seashells ...

So with these other explorations. There is much digression, despite improved techniques. We take our bearings from the wrong landmark, wish that when young we had studied the stars; name the flowers for ourselves and the deserts after others. When the territory is charted, its eventual aspect may be quite other than what was hoped for. One can only say, it will be a whole — a region from which a few features, not necessarily those that seemed prominent at the start, will stand out in clear colours. Not to direct, but to solace us; not to fix our positions, but to show us how we came.

In isolation like this, these final paragraphs might appear rather talky, even platitudinous in their use of landscape to figure the expedition that is Life; but readers have not seemed to find this so. Try the work yourself? Indeed, it would be worthwhile to read both these novels quoted, to see how their authors fill in between their beginning and their ending.

One final reminder. Don't necessarily try to write your beginning, even perhaps with your ending, first up. That might prove the ending of your novel project as well as its beginning!

As elsewhere noted, it's likely you'll not begin writing your novel with its opening anyway. You'll get to that later; which will leave time for your unconscious to work and perhaps produce an appropriate beginning for you. When that time comes, just write it all down freely, without trying to make it fit any of the categories discussed above. It's once you've written those first few paragraphs or pages, that you start checking it out, seeing exactly what you do have and whether that's what you meant to have, and whether it fits with anything you do already have, or have in mind. To be able to understand the nature of what you've done, will help you decide whether it will do the job for you, and how to re-work it if it isn't doing that job. Knowing how these things work is power; and power is control.

6

Dialogue

Talking and eloquence are not the same; to speak, and to speak well, are two things.

BEN JONSON

Despite the fact that dialogue is so important a component of fiction, there are really only a few points to be made about writing it.

First, it is frequently suggested that writers should be listening carefully to everyday speech, to catch its distinctive qualities — its rhythms, patterns, inflections, vocabularies and the like. While this has some merit, it has to be remembered that the everyday speech we hear around us is for the most part quite *un*like written dialogue. Tape-record some, then put it to page; and see.

Morning, Bill. Nice enough sort of day?

Promises to be. You'll be out in the garden, I'd say?

Depends on the wife. She usually shops Thursdays. But Grace is dropping by this week and can only manage the Thursday, so we might have to shop this afternoon instead. How's Mavis?

Still got that damn virus. Can't throw it off. She's on antibiotics now. Affects her appetite. Milk upsets her. Has to miss out on the cornflakes. Complains about that.

Confounded bug hit early this year. No one's had the vaccinations in time. Chap at the office down with it. We're all having to fill in.

It's this long dry spell. Said so on the tele last night. Or it
might have been the Wednesday. That doctor chap's
Wednesday, isn't he?

DIALOGUE TO ADVANCE PLOT

This piece is dreary because its matter is both uninteresting and
repetitive, and its expression pedestrian. Yet it's how folk out
there are doing it. A more important reason the exchange is so
dull and waffly is that it doesn't develop at all, doesn't carry the
episode any further forward. Good dialogue should take you
further along a story's Time Line. If your plot remains, at the end
of a passage of talking, much where it was at the beginning, then
you've not written dialogue at all, just conversation.

Here are two examples of dialogue carrying, and advancing,
plot. The first is from William Mayne's novel for children, IT, and
it displays characterisation and plot momentum, and economy
with language that few authors can match. His use of "said" is
interesting, too; even when it isn't needed for making clear who's
speaking. And never any of the alternative attributions; just "said".
Perhaps this conveys a matter-of-factness, a perfunctoriness, in
Alice's domestic world?

The passage traces an interview with Alice about a reward she
chose to donate to charity.

"I'm from the GAZETTE," said the man. "You must be Alice
Dyson."

"No," said Alice, but she had a feeling that her name had
probably gone wrong forever now. The man took no notice
of her actual words.

"Good," he said. "Understand you found ring belonging Mrs
Willis, Osmington, you properly public spirited, honest, and
Willis came to offer reward, so?"

"Yes," said Alice, when she had worked out what the words
left out of the speech had to be.

"Congratulate," said the man. "GAZETTE small article
picture, permitted?"

"It's neither nowt nor summat," said Dad. "You'll be hard
up for news if that's famous."

"Generous refuse reward offer charity," said the man. "Mrs Willis impressed call office."

"You hear all sorts of tales," said Dad.

"Interesting choose favourite charity," said the man. "Why choose?"

"You've got to like something best," said Alice. "But it wasn't like that at all."

"Smile, stand next mother, nice," said the man, and cracked great lights in her face so that his face turned black when Alice looked at it. "Friday. Going Bishop next part story. How old, Alison? Hobby? Brother- sister?"

"Twelve," said Alice, which was not true yet, and "riding", which wasn't either, and "no brother-sister", which was a lie, not merely untrue.

"Thank," said the man, and went.

"If you tell anyone I'm in the paper," said Alice. "I'll."

The story's progression in the above occurs almost entirely through dialogue.

The second passage is from Shirley Hazard's THE TRANSIT OF VENUS. In it, Caroline Bell is summoned to Mr Leadbetter's office over the matter of Valda Fenchurch's refusal to prepare lunch for the men.

"Miss Fenchchurch has some grievance?"

"She does not like to serve food. It is an imposition."

"And is that not somewhat absurd? The purveying of — ah — victuals being an accepted part of her functions?"

"By whom is it accepted?"

"By every woman here except Miss Fenchurch and, I now take it, yourself. Had there been a wider sense of unfitness, the girls would have expressed it generally."

"Most people have to have unfitness pointed out to them. At first there is usually only one person who does that."

... "And do you not find this a paltry and selfish attitude? The men in this office are, after all, forgoing the lunch hour

> altogether, remaining at the desks for extra duty. The girls
> are merely asked — required — to help them discharge
> onerous extra tasks."

> "The men do nothing that lowers their self-esteem. On the
> contrary, staying at their desks exalts it."

> ....

> Leadbetter's fingers came down on the blotter with a
> synchronised slap. "Miss Bell, do you really not find this
> incident utterly grotesque?"

> "I know that any adherence to a principle can be called
> grotesque, and even made to appear so. At least for a
> time."

> "You call it a principle? A tempest in a tea cup."

At this point Leadbetter sneeringly suggests that, as British ways seem so clearly unsatisfactory to Caroline, she should give serious consideration to returning to New Zealand. Caroline simply replies that she has in fact come to give her resignation.

Note how far the plot has moved on from the beginning of this passage.

MATCHING DIALOGUE WITH CHARACTERS

Second, dialogue should observe decorum — to exhume an eighteenth century term which has a quite different meaning today. That is, dialogue should be appropriate to the person speaking, in terms of social class, occupation, and the like. A farmer should speak like a farmer, not like a wharfie or company director or schoolboy or swaggie or professor. These days, in this part of the world, social differences and their identification through speech and dress and manner are nowhere near as pronounced as they were in eighteenth century Britain. But one still at times sees dialogue where, say, a youth from a shanty town, and one from a school where they have Latin on their blazers, speak pretty much the same.

> "Well it's January and ninety-six in the shade, and we —
> the blokes I mean — are gathering at McGillivray's to wet
> the whistle before the party starts. We're on the verandah,

*see, and maybe some of us on the steps, and some others,
yeah, I reckon some others are under the trees.... We're
talking women, we're talking horses, we're talking bets. Bill
Stolley, the old fool, has just lost his shirt at yesterday's
races and is cadging drinks."*

*"It seems to me," said Lucinda, as she stood watching Paul
arranging figs and greengages in a pretty pottery bowl,
"that all young life is like a crocus, that springs up so
fragile and trusting, and then is trodden on or nipped off
by a sparrow."*

*"I don't think either of us has been very badly trodden on,"
said Paul.*

"I'm not so sure. Anyhow, I was thinking of Stephen."

*"He is much less trodden on than a Welsh miner, for
example... Will you ruin your inside with gin now... or will
you wait and drink some wholesome wine with your
luncheon?"*

*"If I have to wait for more than ten minutes I'll ruin my
inside with gin," said Lucinda, "without prejudice to the
wholesome wine later."*

It is not difficult to decide, from these interchanges, which
speech is upper middle class Anglo-Australian (LUCINDA
BRAYFORD by Martin Boyd) and which is rough Oz (CHARADES
by Janette Turner Hospital).

ATTRIBUTIONS

Third, dialogue almost always contains attributions like *he said*
and *she whispered*. These, of course, should not be used just
automatically, only when there is some specific purpose for
doing so.

Here are two reasons for using attributions. The first is so that
your reader will know who is uttering the words. If this already is
obvious — from the tone, or the content, or because there are
only two characters speaking and the other has just finished —
you might omit attribution altogether. The second reason is that

you wish to communicate additional information to the reader through the *how* of what's being said. For example:

"Take the baby," Derek said, "and sell it."

"Take the baby!" Derek roared, "and sell it!"

"Take the baby," Derek sneered, "and sell it."

"Take the baby," Derek laughed, "and sell it."

"Take the baby," Derek challenged, "and sell it."

Even without any such attributions, you can still convey that Derek is 'the sayer' and communicate quite a deal of additional information at the same time.

"Take the baby!" Derek thrust out the bundle. "Sell it!"

"Take the baby!" Derek flung the bundle. "Sell it!"

"Take the baby." Derek gently, fondly, tweaked tiny Lucy's nose. "Sell it!"

"Take the baby." Derek smiled quizzically down at the red, wrinkled face. "Sell it."

'Take the baby!" Derek stormed away, and flung back over his shoulder — "Sell it!"

Here is a passage where there are few direct attributions at all, yet little doubt about which of the characters is speaking:

They'd overslept. Then because Carmel had several appointments, Peter had dropped the children at the station while she showered. Returned, he'd positioned himself musingly on the edge of the bed.

"Among the richest haps of this post-lapsarian experience," he'd offered benignly, "is a bedroom full of summer light, with gauzy curtains a-billowing ..."

"She'd nodded, bandying legs and towelling in between.

"Your nightwear and yester's garments flung about, as you'd been abducted following some desperate Sabine struggle."

She despatched him a grimace, raised one breast and dabbed.

"A paradise for just idling with the paper. Or marmalade on toast, served crumbs-noir. Or simply dozing and reflecting. Or ... anything, really."

"In your particular case —" She bent to a drawer and
directed a fusillade of underwear towards the bed.
"Especially ANYTHING REALLY/   "

He feigned surprise.

"You're right, of course. Especially ..." He scrutinised her
stooped nakedness with quizzical interest. "Their bosoms
shamed the roses," he quoted then. "Their behinds/
Impelled the astonished nightingales to sing."

"My God!" Carmel straightened. "Is that supposed ... ?"

"Flecker decided not, in the event. James Elroy. He struck it
out."

"Well that's a mercy!" She lifted a dark-blue summer-
weight from the wardrobe, held it up to him questioningly.

"Riding on top!" he informed her promptly. And at her
genuine surprise — "Well, different outfits suggest different
ways of doing it, you know."

"I didn't know, actually."

"And that's indubitably a riding-on-top-of-me ensemble.
Obvious, I'd have thought?"

"Once it's pointed out, of course. Still —" She returned the
suit to the wardrobe "I've no time right now for equestrian
grapplings. Something a little more in the ... doing-it-later
mode. Any configuration you fancy — but later."

She hurried through several combinations and settled
finally on pillar box red with white sleeveless top. Then she
slipped quickly into underwear and began brushing her
hair.

"Hey though!" Peter roused. "Those flimsies? You
co-ordinate all this top finery but step into any old ... You
should try several, and I'll give my ..."

"Peter!" She faced him, hands on hips. "If I start treading in
and out of lingerie in front of you — well, you know!"

"Especially ANYTHING REALLY?"

"I do have appointments."

"In unco-ordinated smalls? Anyway, I didn't even glimpse
... How can I fantasise in the car if I've simply no ... ?"

She hesitated; then lay down the hair brush and turned to
face him and smiled and raised her skirt for his pleasure.

"I suppose I should be all smirky you're so interested. I'd
never make centrefold."

"Light blue." He'd nodded approval. "A fragment of welkin
over Nature's sweetest barley field." He moved closer. "Are
they the kind that ... You know?"

She sighed.

"Let me cancel my first appointment then ..."

Note how in this fond-and-bantering seduction scene, from
STATUES AGAINST THE SKY almost every statement is a bounce
off the preceding statement; or to reverse the point, every
statement provokes a response. Plot is being propelled along its
Time Line too, in that by the final capitulation, events have
moved well on from the initial situation. It is perhaps also worth
remarking that the decorum mentioned earlier is being observed,
in that the male (as would have become apparent before this
point in the story) is a teacher of Eng. Lit.; hence the
sophisticated and sometimes literary tone of the dialogue — and,
indeed, of the narrative carrying it. ("She directed a fusillade of
underwear towards the bed.") The couple are clearly accustomed
to amuse and tease each other by playing with quotation and
literary echo.

LENGTH OF DIALOGUE

Fourth, it is also said about dialogue that long, unbroken
passages by the one speaker are to be avoided. There is some
wisdom in this, particularly for the beginning writer. Such long,
unbroken passages can work well, though, as the fame of many
soliloquies from theatre clearly testify. ("To be or not to be? That
is the question. Whether 'tis better ... ?")

For such long speeches to hold readers, the character doing
the long speech must be conducting some sort of debate,
argument, harangue, as in the passage below. Or outlining some
projected course — how to murder, invade, deceive, escape,
seduce. Or attempting to understand — a suicide, a desertion, a

betrayal, the sacking of some hundreds of miners. Or responding to — theft of the sole remaining koalas in the world; a lover's grief; some challenge. Whatever, there must be tensions involved in what is being declaimed, whether this tension, clash, confrontation is within a divided speaker or between a speaker and a silent listener. Again from STATUES:

"Don't say anything yet Peter. I've got myself calm. I'm prepared to go through it all once more. But finally, this time. So you'll SEE — if you're truly prepared to. Look — I'm breaking bread with you now. Literally. Well, it's a gesture. So? Nothing? As you will then. I'll start from Richard. I could come in from other points, but it's simplest from Richard. And that's what's most immediate. He doesn't know everything about our relationship, but he's well enough aware of its ... intensity. And that makes him difficult. Surly. For example, he won't help about the house. Or rather, he forces me to ask him to do the things he used just to do anyway. Like putting out the garbage, making coffee at breakfast, fetching in the paper. This mightn't sound much, Peter; but it's continual sub-acute hostility. Goading me. And sarcasm. Not particularly subtle, Richard never is. But it does undermine, over the months. He manages to subvert the whole damn running of the house. Everything becomes hassle. And crisis if I don't move at the crouch all the time. And Peter, I do have to get the children off to school every day. Happily, if I can. And to drama lessons. And swimming classes. And shop and keep petrol in the car and clean clothes and food in the fridge and meals on time. Plus holding down my job; and parents carrying on every opportunity. And this isn't just hysteria, Peter. I simply can't cope much longer. It's not only you, I concede that. Richard's resentful because he intuits that I'm not able to be ... well, proud of him any more. This will sound terribly confused; but it torments me to see him so full of ... well, I suppose it's fear. Some kind of sense of dispossession. I'm to blame for a lot of that, I know. But I can't even think clearly with all these complications from you. These ... waves. Peter, Richard is a strong man. He goes out, gets what he wants. For me too. People respect him. I assumed he'd front up, fight to keep me. But he doesn't, not any more. He just retreats, and snipes. Fills our

house with resentments. *He's been disabled. Even the*
occasional violence, I see that as ... I realise now that he
must have drawn some kind of strength from our
marriage. And Peter — my children, he is their father.
Absurdly Edwardian, I know; but it does count for
something with women. Some women anyway. And ... and
that's far from all that distresses me. In fact it's not even
the most important. But I find it increasingly impossible to
... survive with. Peter? Peter — do you understand this
much?"

One final word about dialogue. There are conventions for its punctuation, and some Guides will outline these. Of late decades, however, dialogue has come to be punctuated in a variety of ways, but it seems most sensible just to stay with what is traditional.

7

Imagery

Sleepe is the image of death.

ANON 1620

Every writer of fiction, indeed every user of words, employs imagery — even those with only the vaguest notion of what that term means. An understanding of the way imagery works, and skill in its use, will make your writing more vivid, more moving, and often more resonating.

So, what is imagery?

You will find definitions in dictionaries of literary terms, and chapters, even whole tomes, devoted to discussing the topic. Not all will be of very practical use to the writer.

Here's one simple way to approach the subject:

Language, which is the resource material of imagery, seems to communicate in at least three ways. First, it presents directly. There's a one-to-one correspondence of a particular *word* to whatever that word *designates*. 'Sweep', for example, is what you do with a broom on the floor. 'Breeze' is a light wind; 'gust', a burst of wind. 'Brown' is the colour of a material object; while 'walk' is putting one leg in front of the other in front of the other in front of ... in order to move forward.

These five words, however, can be used in quite another way, in an extended way — to suggest something entirely beyond these direct, one-to-one meanings.

Nyra's eyes SWEPT the room.

84

Carmel BREEZED through the door,GUSTING up smiles and
greetings from the guests.

A little man with a dark BROWN voice.

"I can still WALK my wits somewhat," Pirin noted drily.

Now, Nyra's eyes didn't really get down to floor level and deal
with detritus there. Nor is Carmel the name of a couple of
manifestations of wind. Voices don't have colour; and whatever
wits are, they're indubitably legless! (Nor, for that matter, can
speech be wet or dry.)

There is, however, something in the act of sweeping that
conveys the way Nyra's eyes looked around that room. 'Breezed'
and 'gusting' do invoke a good deal of the very cheery and
energetic entrance Carmel made. Colour does suggest qualities
that it cannot literally attach to — one's spirits can be black or
grey (or even blue!); one can see red, wish golden days, be green
either in years or with envy, or a cowardly yellow or quite
browned off or write purple prose. And walking must catch up
something about exercising the reason — 'walking wits' —
because even in explaining this use a physical-movement word,
"exercising", has been resorted to.

This way of using language is termed 'metaphoric', and it is
employed to reveal or create likeness between things. We, as
writers, employ metaphor to make vivid, to present something
freshly, to evoke feeling; to paint word pictures. Here are some
further examples:

➤ The moon smiled over the hedge like a smug farmer.

➤ Not even the rain has such small feet.

➤ Loose as the wind.

➤ Your body's whitest song.

➤ The ragged meadow of my soul.

➤ Her lips cherries, her hair spun sunlight, her cheeks roses..

➤ Her eyes, great love crumbs.

➤ Appetite, the universal wolf.

This kind of imagery, which renders vivid, is the stock-in-
trade of successful fiction writers. They use it to create

background, heighten action, fetch characters to life, and generally to give us lively, colourful prose.

There is a third way in which imagery uses items from the external world. This is to transmit to us the inner states of characters — a sort of visible landscape to suggest the interior topography of those characters — which interior landscapes are not, of course, directly visible. This kind of imagery can equally well be used to carry and express themes.

An example of the first use, transmitting the inner states of characters, occurs in: "My life ... is fall'n into the sere, the yellow leaf." This is Shakespeare's Macbeth, when he realises that murdering for the crown has lost him all that was most precious in his life — his wife, troops of friends and their golden opinions. (There's another, 'golden'!). A casebook statement of Macbeth's despair (clinical depression?) would take many pages and of course have its own truth and value; but Shakespeare's brief autumnal image catches the descent into desolation and communicates this to us in ten words.

An example of imagery revealing and communicating themes is the wild storm that breaks over King Lear on the heath. This isn't simply some meteorological phenomenon, nor just supportive background and atmosphere. It is, first of everything, a dramatic externalising of the tempest raging within that tormented King's breast.

> Blow, winds, and crack your cheeks. Rage, blow.
> You cataracts and hurricanoes, spout
> Till you have drenched our steeples, drowned the cocks.
> You sulph'rous and thought-executing fires,
> Vaunt couriers of oak-cleaving thunderbolts,
> Singe my white head. And thou, all-shaking thunder,
> Strike flat the thick rotundity o' the world ...

Try reading it shouting, bellowing; shaking your fists at heaven. Well, that's what it was like inside that enraged, forsaken (and entirely self-pitying) King Lear.

Before launching into an extended exploration of imagery as a device for energising, deepening and enriching your fiction, here are two specific points:

First, not everyone will be looking to employ lots of imagery in his/her work. Jane Austen didn't go in for it to any great extent, though there is perhaps more in MANSFIELD PARK and PERSUASION than in the other novels. One might be tempted to assert that imagery tends to accompany fiction of the heart rather than of the head; only if one did, clever people would start flooding the exceptions in!

Second, imagery doesn't necessarily have to be planned, be deliberate. Indeed, most of this third kind of imagery in fiction — inner states, and themes — probably just happens courtesy of the author's subconscious. For example, it seems very unlikely that Shakespeare sat down and meditated thus:

> *Now I want to write a play about these two youngsters*
> *whose love flares up so sudden and intense that its own*
> *flames consume it. So to suggest something of this whole*
> *idea, I'll get in a falling star that blazes and burns out on*
> *the instant; and quarrels flaring up in the hot street with*
> *sudden killing, and ..*

That, however, is how ROMEO AND JULIET in fact turned out. You will likely find, then, that in your writing, imagery will often suggest itself, emerge intuitively as you choose your settings and crank up atmosphere. So, you need settings that will in turn work for you. Your great love scene wouldn't have much of a chance, for example, if you set it in the offal room of a slaughterhouse! Only Woody Allen could bring that off!

IMAGERY AT WORK

Now to imagery at work, with WUTHERING HEIGHTS as the source of example. There are a number of image clusters here, among which are:

➤ Imagery from the natural world.

➤ Imagery of enclosure and escape.

➤ Window imagery.

➤ Imagery in the final paragraphs.

Imagery from the Natural World

The first, and most obvious, is imagery from the natural world. One of the main ways we are made to feel the power of the Cathy and Heathcliff love, is through the novel's setting. Their love is like the moors themselves — free, natural, elemental; at times serene, more often tempestuous. How differently we would feel about their relationship if Cathy spent her days at Daphne's Kiddies Comics Mart, and Heathcliff was a detergent salesman from Clacton-on-Sea! Even the novel's title catches up something of the fierceness of the children of that wuthering/withering/weathering house. If the title were DINGLEY DELL or THE WOMBAT'S REST ...? Indeed, a complete approach to the novel has been constructed around the two houses as landscape:

> On the one hand we have "Wuthering Heights", the land of
> the storm; high on the barren moorland, naked to the
> shock of the elements, the natural home of the Earnshaw
> family, fiery, untamed children of the storm. On the other,
> sheltered in the leafy valley below, stands "Thrushcross
> Grange", the appropriate home of the children of calm, the
> gentle, passive, timid Lintons.

David Cecil in EARLY VICTORIAN NOVELISTS goes on to explain the action of WUTHERING HEIGHTS in terms of the two houses as landscape. Opposed, the two bring destruction down upon their whole world. But in harmony, as in the love of Hareton and Catherine ...

Another writer, Dorothy Van Ghent, points out much the same thing in THE ENGLISH NOVEL: FORM AND FUNCTION:

> ... the violent figures of Catherine and Heathcliff, portions
> of the flux of nature, children of rock and heath and
> tempest ...

Even in her natural world's bits-of-business, Emily Bronte can communicate to us something about her characters and their situations. Take this brief description of the immediate surrounds of "Wuthering Heights":

> ... one may guess the power of the north wind blowing over
> the edge, by the excessive slant of a few stunted firs at the
> end of the house; and by a range of gaunt thorns all
> stretching their limbs one way, as if craving alms of the
> sun.

Primarily descriptive lines, of course; and yet quite evocative of Heathcliff and his situation too? He has, as a human individual, been blown on by the powerful north wind of rejection, of brutal treatment. He might be said to have developed an excessive slant, a distortion emotionally. He is certainly like a gaunt thorn! And his limbs do all stretch one way — to Catherine, his sun.

If this reading of 'simple description' should seem somewhat too ingenious — then look at these lines later in the novel: Heathcliff to Hareton:

> Now, my bonny lad, you are mine. And we'll see whether one tree won't grow as crooked as another, with the same wind to twist it.

The very same imagery, but this time being used explicitly for the purpose suggested for the earlier passage.

So, the natural world, used 'imagistically', can very effectively transmit inner states of emotion and attitude. Indeed we do it all the time, out in the full stream (*the full stream?*) of our workaday world. A shower of tears; the Spring of life; golden oldies; my heart is a desert; vast deserts of eternity; the sunshine of your smile; the twilight of life; winter in her gaze, or in her bones; starry-eyed; More fairer been thy brestes than is wyn (that's Chaucer!); the flower of civilisation; a piercing gaze; Extinction's Alp.

If we don't exploit these possibilities in our fiction — have the day cloud over suddenly, say, as the harbinger of bad news — then we are dispossessing ourselves of one of the most potent means of intensifying our writing and its impact on our readers.

Enclosure and Escape

Imagery of enclosure and escape in WUTHERING HEIGHTS could also be expressed as imagery of imprisonment and liberty; and even of inside and outside, as the novel is full of people who are inside trying to get out, or outside trying to get in!

As children, Cathy and Heathcliff try to escape the tyranny of Hindley and Joseph by running *outside* onto the moors; and this position is later reversed when in Lockwood's nightmare, Cathy's spirit clamours to get *inside* through the latticed window. Lockwood, however, bars her *out*. Heathcliff then, in "an uncontrollable passion of tears", begs her to come *in*. (Lockwood at this early point is himself imprisoned *inside* "Wuthering Heights" — snowbound!) Also, Isabella and the second Catherine each escape from Heathcliff and the Heights — Isabella to a kind of freedom, Cathy hardly so.

Less obvious, though, are the imprisonments and escapes that are not physical. For example, Cathy's marriage to Edgar is a kind of escape — from poverty and uncouthness, to affluence and the social graces. And Heathcliff might be seen as imprisoned within his obsession for vengeance ... which he escapes, finally, through death. Several characters are imprisoned by their pasts, which they try to escape by fleeing from one place, or from one person, to another.

Even those final graves represent a kind of escape for the three characters of the love triangle — escape from the constraints and censures of society and religion. They are sited outside both the village, and the churchyard.

The very bric-a-brac of the novel draws our attention to these concerns, by having locks and keys, and lock-and-key incidents, throughout. Indeed, it might be hard to find another novel that has so many struggles over keys, so much smashing of locks or scaling of walls, of slipping through windows.

This recurring suggestiveness is itself a kind of imagery. The locks and keys are more than just plot devices, or items of 'furniture', within the novel. They direct us to themes and issues, as outlined above.

Window Imagery

It's not possible to be so precise about window imagery; but Emily Bronte does seem to use windows to suggest something of the visibility one-to-the-other of the novel's two worlds, and the fragility of the threshold between them. That is, the world of the Grange, of restraint and the cultivated, is very visible to Catherine from where she is in the world of the Heights, of natural impulse and of passion.

Catherine and Heathcliff as children see the world of the Grange through a window as they crouch in the dark outside. Cathy is tempted by what she sees; and smashes the window to get inside. Not literally smashes, of course; though Heathcliff uses that very image when he declares:

> ... if Catherine had wished to return, I intended shattering
> their great glass panes to a million fragments, unless they
> let her out.

And indeed, this is something of what he does in fact do as an adult, when he returns from his mysterious absence away in the world — smash the visible barriers between his natural world and the Grange world of social order. He finds Catherine and Edgar seated by a window, that very point of threshold and clash, where Cathy attempts to mediate between them. Throughout the crisis which follows, Cathy keeps asking Nelly to open the window — her escape route back into Heathcliff's world. This is intensified during her final illness:

> Open the window again wide, fasten it open! Quick, why
> don't you move?

It is from this open window that she "catches her death"; and indeed she threatens to kill herself by a "spring from the window". This gets echoed by her subsequent "spring" into Heathcliff's arms.

After that, she never regains consciousness. That first passing "through the window" from the moorland world into the Grange, from Heathcliff's world to Edgar's, proved ultimately fatal to her.

Heathcliff then takes leave of her corpse — significantly, by climbing back *through the window* from her adopted world. After Cathy's funeral, he returns to the Heights and enters the building by smashing through windows! And later, as Heathcliff himself slides towards death, he increasingly seeks to be at windows, to look out.

When Heathcliff dies, Nelly discovers "the master's window swinging open, the rain driving straight in." His hand rests on the sill, with blood trickling from it. This takes the reader back to the child-wraith Cathy reaching in through a window, blood likewise flowing (from slashed wrists). Nelly finally proceeds to close Heathcliff's window; but, she tells us, she can't close his eyes — those windows of the soul!

The younger Catherine, by the way, has little trouble with windows. She slips easily in and out of them at both the Grange and the Heights.

It's not surprising, then, that she is the one finally able to unite the two houses — the barriers hardly exist for her. The young and sickly Linton Heathcliff, however, dislikes windows; and his influence on events is a divisive one.

Final Paragraph Imagery

Perhaps most important of all, because it determines our final reading of this novel — the imagery of the final paragraphs. Here they are:

> My walk home was lengthened by a diversion in the direction of the kirk. When beneath its walls, I perceived decay had made progress, even in seven months: many a window showed black gaps deprived of glass; and slates jutted off, here and there, beyond the right line of the roof, to be gradually worked off in coming autumn storms.

> I sought, and soon discovered, the three headstones on the slope next the moor: the middle one grey, and half buried in heath: Edgar Linton's only harmonised by the turf and moss creeping up its foot: Heathcliff's still bare.

> I lingered round them, under that benign sky; watched the moths fluttering among the heath and harebells, listened to the soft wind breathing through the grass, and wondered how anyone could ever imagine unquiet slumbers for the sleepers in that quiet earth.

Most readers, probably, have been satisfied to read this as positive ending. At the very least, they would see those desperate three as now at peace. It is usually claimed, too, that Heathcliff and his Catherine have been united again beyond the grave. If you ask the more informed and articulate of these readers why they understand the novel's ending thus, they would likely point to the natural imagery there of tranquillity restored — "moths fluttering" amongst "heath" and "harebells" in "soft wind" under a "benign sky".

There are, though, a few readers who have felt some problems with this. The first is that the words in the final paragraphs are not the author's, but the narrator Lockwood's. He's really giving it to us the way he's seeing it. And knowing what we do of Lockwood's inadequacy in understanding matters of the heart, can we be entirely satisfied with his summing up? Indeed, Emily Bronte has made the beginning of the novel full of Lockwood's mini-mistakings — as a forewarning, perhaps?

Heathcliff is "a capital fellow", the cushion of kittens on the chair turns out to be dead rabbits, the second Catherine proves not to be Heathcliff's wife at all. What great confidence then does the author allow us in Lockwood's judgement at that critical, summing up point of the novel?

If you look again at this imagery of the natural world, though, you might see it as not so convincingly supporting Lockwood's upbeat and somewhat sentimental view. Certainly the soft winds and benign sky and flower-sprinkled earth are there; but so are their contraries.

Against the soft winds are posed autumn gales. As well as the benign sky, there is a disintegrating roof. The flower-sprinkled earth coexists with three graves in process of obliteration. The very way these items of imagery are linked in balance one against the other, surely demands that we see them coupled and opposed like this?

What we have, then, is Lockwood's voice describing the scene; but Emily Bronte behind that voice, making the initial selection of imagery.

Lockwood draws attention to the images that suggest quiet slumbers for sleepers in a quiet earth. He ignores the significance of those coexisting images that might direct us to an alternative and harsher reading of the novel's outcome. That is, it isn't really at all self-evident that Heathcliff's and Cathy's love was so great and wonderful that it survived death. Rather, perhaps, they had their chance, but through betrayal and violent hatreds, they dropped it. Death offers them neither reunion nor restitution; only eternal annihilation. "Ashes", as one reader put it.

You will fetch your own response to the ending of this novel; but it is worth noting that a harsh ending certainly would not run against anything else in the work, encompassing as this novel does, wife bashing and child abuse — if not child murder!

Cathy's deathbed scene, for example, might well be the most brutal in nineteenth century fiction. Emily Bronte could have had Cathy reject Heathcliff at this point, so that marriage vows triumph and Heathcliff is punished for his adulterous behaviour. The great middle class reading public would have endorsed such a scene. Or, the pair could have joined in a kind of Byronic defiance of social mores, the world well lost for love.

Bronte goes neither of these ways. Instead, she has Heathcliff savage the dying Catherine with a terrifying analysis of her behaviour:

> ... *she put her hand to clasp his neck, and bring her cheek to his as he held her; while he, in return, covering her with frantic caresses, said wildly:*

> *"... Why did you betray your own heart, Cathy? I have not one word of comfort. You deserve this. You have killed yourself. Yes, you may kiss me, and cry; and wring out my kisses and tears: they'll blight you — they'll damn you. You loved me — then what RIGHT had you to leave me? What right — answer me — for the poor fancy you felt for Linton? Because misery and degradation, and death, and nothing that God or Satan could inflict could have parted us, YOU , of your own will, did it.*

> *I have not broken your heart — YOU have broken it; and in breaking it, you have broken mine ..."*

> *"Leave me alone. Leave me alone," sobbed Catherine. "If I have done wrong, I am dying for it ..."*

This is quite shatteringly realistic, and along with the harsher imagery noted, should make us wary of too readily accepting Lockwood's soft conclusion.

It will be hardly necessary to point out that unless you have the writing skills — genius? — of novelists like Emily Bronte, you will hardly be looking to enrich your work with such complex patterns of imagery. But this analysis demonstrates just what can be gained from imagery and suggests ways of going about exploiting what it offers.

Imagery and Setting

It will probably have become apparent to you that imagery is closely linked with setting, atmosphere and even tone. So a description of a harsh, bleak landscape, rendered in a forthright, uncompromising tone, might well produce an atmosphere that seemed to challenge human aspiration or stifle human endeavour.

Occasionally atmosphere and setting are made to contrast with rather than offer support within a story, as with the hypothetical Woody Allen example earlier; or, a couple mud-splattered and rain-drenched, hugging and laughing; or violent rape and murder on an idyllic tropical beach. The effect of such contrasts can be comic; or it can act to emphasise that the dreadful coexists with the wonderful; or it can challenge, destabilise; or it can emphasise. At such a point it gets almost impossible to disentangle setting, atmosphere, imagery and perhaps tone.

Most writers instinctively choose an appropriate setting, one which will work for them; and blend this with an equally appropriate narrative tone; and thus have atmosphere and a source for imagery. So, a grey, rainy day for a funeral scene; a stormy night for violence; a hard, fractured prose for colliding human aspirations in a crowded city; a deeply dark night for bafflement of the soul; sunset for farewell and departure and loss.

The whole first chapter of Thomas Hardy's THE RETURN OF THE NATIVE, given over to a description of Egdon Heath, combines atmosphere, tone and theme very effectively. Here are the first two paragraphs subtitled, "A Face on which Time makes but Little Impression":

A Saturday afternoon in November was approaching the time of twilight, and the vast tract of unenclosed wild known as Egdon Heath embrowned itself moment by moment. Overhead the hollow stretch of whitish cloud shutting out the sky was as a tent which had the whole heath for its floor.

The heaven being spread with this pallid screen and the earth with the darkest vegetation, their meeting-line at the horizon was clearly marked. In such contrast the heath wore the appearance of an instalment of night which had taken up its place before its astronomical hour was come ... The face of the heath by its mere complexion added half an hour to evening; it could in like manner retard the dawn, sadden noon, anticipate the frowning of storms scarcely generated, and intensify the opacity of a moonless midnight to a cause of shaking and dread.

This very dark opening to the novel sets the scene for a story in which the characters get themselves involved in tragic situations. They are presented as vulnerable to hurt and to disaster; as walking into an almost waiting "night" of their own making, from which they cannot escape.

Early in the novel, Olly Dowden, one of the "rustics", says pityingly of another character — "Poor little thing, her feelings got the better of her, no doubt. 'Tis nature"; and then a little later, she adds — "And what's done cannot be undone."

These lines enunciate explicitly what the opening account of Egdon Heath broodingly suggests: that actions have consequences which follow them as inevitably as night follows day; and that such consequences cannot be escaped, however much a victim might try to reverse the earlier, fateful action.

The "native" who returns at the beginning of this novel is Clym Yeobright. Somewhat to the locals' amazement, Yeobright has abandoned Paris and his diamond business of many years, choosing instead to come home to the heath.

Clym's return involves him in a situation with potentially disastrous consequences, and these not only for himself. His nature is idealistic and noble, but also passionate and sensuous; and he falls in love with the beautiful, romantic and unhappy Eustacia Vye. She responds to Clym because she believes he will take her away from the Heath; which is just the one thing, of course, he will not want to do for her! An inescapably destructive outcome is thus programmed.

Through his setting, Hardy has created the scene for this human conflict. While Egdon Heath, a made-up name for one of the great windswept heathlands of south-west England, magnifies the conflict in some ways by foregrounding it against such a seamless backdrop, it also very much reduces it; because the Heath is so vast and so timeless that human beings are seen as minute against its perspective.

> This obscure, obsolete, superseded country figures in
> Domesday. Its condition is recorded therein as that of
> heathy, furzy, briary wilderness ... The great inviolate place
> had an ancient permanence which the sea cannot claim.
> Who can say of a particular sea that it is old? Distilled by
> the sun, kneaded by the moon, it is renewed in a year, in a
> day, or in an hour. The sea changed, the fields changed,
> the rivers, the villages, and the people changed, yet Egdon
> remained.

Not only does this kind of perspective show the individual human as ephemeral, as insignificant when you consider all who have passed through life since earth began. It is also used by Hardy to project the whole issue of individuals pitting themselves against their natural world, against the elemental; which is, of course, one of the oldest preoccupations in literature.

There is also a sense that human beings are traversing routes familiar to all those who have gone before. Such routes of course are not only literally roads but the psychic paths that people follow in search of love and happiness, peace and fulfilment; though often finding none of these.

> The above-mentioned highway traversed the lower levels of
> the heath, from one horizon to another. In many portions
> of its course it overlaid an old vicinal way, which branched
> from the great Western road of the Romans ... hard by. On
> the evening under consideration it would have been
> noticed that, though the gloom had increased sufficiently
> to confuse the minor features of the heath, the white
> surface of the road remained almost as clear as ever.

You can see how Hardy has used his imagery in this passage to reinforce many of the novel's points. Human life can be difficult. But countless others have already endured that pilgrimage. So despite the gloom, the way to be travelled is as clear as ever; and this is the road the characters are to follow, the path of all generations before. Human desires and aspirations, their passions, needs and satisfactions, are as they always were; and so are the difficulties and implacabilities of the life experience, as imaged in Egdon Heath. Note, too, that the road traverses the Heath's lower levels; perhaps suggesting this is the safest, if more limited, way of negotiating life — keeping to the manageable levels of engagement, inter-meshing. Eustacia, perhaps significantly, is mainly associated with the heights of the Heath. Clym, as a native, seems linked with both heights and depths, and with the levels as well.

Probably the image of Egdon Heath works so well in the novel, looms over it and permeates its action, because it is so economically integrated with character, theme and plot. That is, as we've seen, setting doesn't serve just the one function — as, say, the Egdon-versus-Paris plot component. Hardy uses it to bring out and explore significances in many areas of the novel.

An awareness of, and an understanding of, these techniques relating to imagery, should enable you to lift the quality of your own writing, and to link with readers at a deeper level than any solely documenting kind of writing would enable you to do.

8

$\mathcal{N}$arrators & $\mathcal{N}$arrating

Point-of-view isn't an optional extra in a story. Every
piece of writing, no matter how neutral it seems, has a
point-of-view.

THE WRITING BOOK Kate Grenville

Narrating ... is telling the story. The narrator is the one
who does this telling. There can, of course, be several
tellers of the one story — hence multiple narrators.

As a writer, you can make your narrating as simple, or as
complex, as you wish. Generally speaking, though, the simpler
you have it, the easier it will be to handle. Some of the most
powerful fiction, however, owes a considerable part of this
power to a quite involved and demanding-on-the-reader vehicle
of narration. WUTHERING HEIGHTS, as we'll presently see, is
one such.

There are two basic ways of getting your story told; two main
kinds of narration.

The teller-of-the-story can be a character within that story as
he/she tells it. For example:

*My name is Robert, and I happened to be wandering down
by the Harbour that June Sunday when I suddenly ...*

This is first person narration, the speaker-narrator writing
from within the story, as 'I'.

The author can also, however, be someone quite outside the
events he/she is narrating. That is, this he/she is sitting at a desk

somewhere, making-it-all-up on a typewriter or word processor or whatever. This is third person narration, with the narrator writing not as 'I', but about 'he' and 'she' and 'it'.

> Her name is Roberta and she happened to be wandering down by the Harbour that June Sunday when she suddenly...

FIRST PERSON NARRATOR

We will start with the first person narrator, the 'I'. This 'I' tends to be either a central-to-the-story 'I', or a somewhat-outside-the-story 'I'. A central-to-the-story 'I' would be heavily involved in the story — indeed, quite likely the principal character, as Holden is in CATCHER and Sara Munday is in HERSELF SURPRISED. You could have a tough cop narrating his own investigation; a romantic heroine tracing her journey to happiness-ever-after (as Jane Eyre); or an old person looking back in TIRRA LIRRA BY THE RIVER; or an adolescent who decides to buck the drug world (as in a number of US 'young adult' novels).

On the other hand, the narrating 'I' could be a character more out on the fringe of the story; someone who is really only witnessing the events and recording them; who is probably also commenting on them; and perhaps even evaluating them. Dr Watson in the Sherlock Holmes detective stories would for the most part come into this category; and the narrator Lockwood in WUTHERING HEIGHTS certainly so.

Even Dowell, in THE GOOD SOLDIER, might claim a niche here too, in the sense that although as the betrayed husband he has a central role in plot terms, it isn't really Dowell's fate that the reader becomes involved with. He's not "the good soldier", that exemplary English gentleman Edward Ashburnam who, it is gradually revealed, has over nine years been engaged in secret and of course treacherous adultery with his close friend's wife! Dowell's importance, for the reader, is more in his role as narrator and evaluator of these events.

EXAMPLES OF FIRST PERSON NARRATOR

To convey these differences, here are several examples of first person narration. The most straightforward is from Janet Frame's autobiography, Vol. 3, THE ENVOY FROM MIRROR CITY. It simply chronicles events and the narrator's immediate responses to those, with no attempt to dress anything up, to suggest any wider significances. The passage, though, does have some particular interest for us, as it is about our present topic of writing.

> In my room in the new flat I again began my life as a writer, sitting each morning trying to type while I stared at the oppressive brick walls of Kentish Town. And each week I kept an appointment at the Maudsley Hospital with Dr Miller, each time realising with growing gloom that his departure was weeks away, and when one day he introduced me to his replacement, a Dr Portion, I felt my heart sinking as I heard the crisp English accent contrasting so strangely with Dr Miller's rich cheerful voice with its accent that I had known for years, in Hollywood films. I wondered how I could possibly talk to Dr Portion.

Somewhat similarly, though with a different tone, is Sara Munday in HERSELF SURPRISED telling the story in which she is the central character — her lifelong stormy and stop-start relationship with the wildly eccentric painter Gulley Jimson.

> Gulley was always reading Blake, who was a poet about a hundred years ago, and illustrated his own poems. I think Gulley agreed very well with Blake when he told me Blake used to play Adam and Eve with his poor wife, and draw her too. Once he threatened to take two wives and he always claimed the right, and this was like Gulley, who used to argue that it would not matter to me if he had another woman so long as she did not interfere with me or my pleasure. So I would tell him that if he meant Rozzie, he might try, but I didn't think he would succeed, and if he did, it would be the end of him. For Rozzie was a man-killer and had killed her own husband.

An example of a first person narrator who is right out on the periphery of the story he tells, is Emily Bronte's Mr Lockwood.

Lockwood is the only direct narrator in the story. Every single word of it comes through him, one way or another. Yet, he witnesses personally only a small part of the whole story, and is involved only peripherally in much of that small part.

So where does he get this story from, that he passes on to readers? Well, most of it is told to him by the servant, Nelly Dean.

She was involved in quite a deal of it, though certainly not all. A little of the story comes from the servant Zillah, a mite more from Dr Kenneth; and some through a journal, through words carved above a door, and even from a ghost! Some of this gets told to Nelly, who tells it to Lockwood, who tells it to us.

So not only do the events come to us third or even fourth hand, with the kinds of problems that creates about how much confidence one can have in the accuracy and adequacy of what is (eventually) passed on to us; but Lockwood must seem about the very worst narrator an author could have chosen for this particular story. He knows little about the inhabitants of the Yorkshire Moors, and even less about the kinds of passional experiences he is chronicling. Indeed, his only 'love' episode appears to have been some trading-of-glances with a young woman at a seaside resort — and then taking flight when that young woman at length began tentatively responding! Reasons for Bronte's seemingly strange choice of narrator, are suggested elsewhere.

So, despite Lockwood's undoubted honesty and his determination to get to the bottom of the whole story, he is actually an inadequate narrator. Which indicates another decision an author employing first person narration has to make: how reliable is to be that narrator's testimony? The unreliable narrator can give complex and even gripping effects; but is difficult to manage. The more reliable narrator, like Holden and Dante and Sarah Munday, is probably safer for the less experienced. Though even with such dependable narrators, there can emerge qualifications. Holden's age, for instance, leads him to miss certain significances and nuances; and he tends to see things somewhat in black-and-white, perhaps?

Many eighteenth and nineteenth century authors, like Henry Fielding and George Eliot, achieved an effect of complete reliability by making an appearance, as the author, in their own novels. George Eliot opens her ADAM BEDE thus:

> With a single drop of ink for a mirror, the Egyptian sorcerer undertakes to reveal to any chance comer far- reaching visions of the past. This is what I undertake to do for you, reader. With this drop of ink at the end of my pen I will show you the roomy workshop of Mr Jonathan Burge, carpenter and builder in the village of Hayslope, as it appeared on the eighteenth of June, in the year of our Lord 1799.

Readers today probably find such an authorial approach wordy and old-fashioned. It does though promote a sense of authenticity.

ADVANTAGES OF FIRST PERSON NARRATOR

You will see, then, that to write in the first person, either as primary participant or in the distanced role of observer, offers an author several distinct opportunities and advantages.

For a start, there arises from such writing a strong sense of immediacy, of closeness to the events, of everything being first hand. The writer was *there;* eyewitness at least; and very often, a central experiencer in the thick of it. This in turn confers authority on the narration, making for convincingness.

Additionally, first person narration allows a good deal of the story's action to take place inside the head of the narrator.

That is, the reader is directly plugged in to a consciousness — the narrator's thoughts and feelings — 'I thought' and 'I felt'. And this occurs, for the most part, when these thoughts and feelings are actually happening — even if happening only in retrospect.

Some feel, too, that first person narration tends to have greater pace, of narrative momentum generally. This is partly due to the way such a narrator can imbue the reader with a strong sense of pursuing and discovering, when the narrator is him/herself involved in some kind of quest — to explain a baffling complex of events, for example; or to track down some individual lost or in hiding; or to reach some achievement goal.

Mr Lockwood again provides an example of this. He visits that stark moorland house, finds it full of mystery and strange violences which climax when, on a night of "one bitter whirl of wind and suffocating snow" the wraith of the child Catherine sobs at his latticed window to be let in, and Mr Heathcliff, in "an uncontrollable passion of tears", flings himself to this window and cries — "Come in! Come in! Cathy, do come. Oh do — once more! Oh! my heart's darling! Hear me this time, Catherine, at last!"

Lockwood leaves "Wuthering Heights" very much wanting to find out what's going on. As we readers also want to know. And Lockwood's wanting-to-know, as he begins to find out more and more, resolves itself into two questions:

1. How did things get to be like this in the first place? That is, how did it all begin?

2. How does everything work out from this point on? That is, how does it all conclude?

These are precisely the questions we readers would be asking. Hence we become involved with Lockwood in his quest, and he might be seen as in a way our rep. in the novel, asking our questions, digging around on our behalf. This forces us, like Lockwood and along with Lockwood, to try to assess whatever is discovered about the characters and their behaviour.

For example, did Cathy really marry Edgar Linton so she would be able to help Heathcliff, as she claims to Nelly? Or is this just a cover-up for more mercenary and self-interested motives? Read the pages: Nelly anyway seems not too convinced by Cathy's protestations. But then how percipient is Nelly, in a matter like this? Is Nelly, in fact, biased in her account generally — particularly biased against Heathcliff? Are her judgements about Heathcliff fair and accurate? (She seems to have no understanding of his final fasting and decline and death.) Lockwood, a stranger, can hardly answer such questions for us. Anyway, all this querying and sifting acts to precipitate us as readers almost into the novel itself, as if we were Honorary Characters there, interacting directly with Bronte's own imagined characters.

These then are some of the advantages that first person narration offers, and you will be able to consider them in relation to your own work-in-progress or in-prospect.

DISADVANTAGES OF FIRST PERSON NARRATOR

Where you have advantages, however, you can expect disadvantages too. It will be obvious that, with most first person narration, the narrating 'I' can have no direct access to the minds and hearts of other characters in the tale. Those other characters can tell the narrating 'I' what they are thinking and feeling, or tell others who in turn will pass it all on to that 'I'. Or, the 'I' can try working it out from external evidences like facial expressions or particular actions. Such devices, however, mostly prove clumsy and unconvincing.

All this, of course, is disadvantage only if the first person narrator needs, for the plot, to be able to tap other consciousnesses in his tale. Your story, though, might depend quite directly on the narrator *not* knowing vital plot elements. Not knowing who is telling truth, say; so that the story becomes a quest to find out. Not knowing who loves (or hates) whom; whose character is likely to prove the most enduring under stress. The limitation of not-knowing would be working for you in such circumstances.

QUALITIES OF THE FIRST PERSON NARRATOR

One final point about first person narrating: such a narrator needs to be interesting either in his/her own right; or at least, interesting because of the nature of the situation he/she is in.

With the former — 'interesting in his/her own right' — the engaging quality would of course be part of the character's personality. So it is that Holden Caulfield, despite his sometimes shallow judgements and hasty intolerance of anything striking him as "phoney" and some irritating repetitiveness with his speech idioms ... so it is that Holden grabs us through his energy and his fresh and often challenging ways of responding to experiences, and his underlying strong humanity. He can really sum things up — as, dismissively, by simply saying — "just like the goddam movies". Holden, it is revealed several times, is very good at composition, with English his top subject. It's entirely believable, then, that he "writes" so well.

On the other hand the first person narrator is, as we've seen, often quite the opposite to the above — a rather limited character who possesses nothing very special in the way of writing skills. The interest attaching to such a narrator must come then from the situations in which that narrator finds him/herself. Lockwood struggling to unravel the mysteries associated with "Wuthering Heights", is one such. Dr Watson trying to unravel not only Sherlock Holmes' mysteries, but Dr Holmes himself, is another.

It is worth looking for a moment at this Holmes-Watson paradigm, as it seems a common one — up to a point, 'straight guy and fall guy'. Two reasons why this combination is so successful might be:

1. If we were privy to Holmes' consciousness throughout the stories, then we'd be able to follow his reasonings as they were occurring; so there'd be little mystery and no surprises.

2. Again, an inadequate narrator gives the reader a rep. within the tale; one who shares our bafflements, asks our questions, experiences our surprises.

These considerations all apply, by and large, whether the first person narrator is at the centre of his/her story or out on the periphery.

MULTIPLE NARRATORS

The obvious difficulty, already noted, of the 'I' author's dealing with events from which he/she was absent, can arise less if you are using multiple first person narrators — that is, two or more narrating 'I's. Bronte, as we saw, does this in WUTHERING HEIGHTS, so that a group of people (Lockwood, Nelly and Zillah), or devices (like the child Catherine's journal) more or less pool their individual 'I' experiences.

More straightforward and less tricky would be to have two or three narrators each telling a different and entirely separate part of a story; and not telling to each other, but directly to the reader.

This sort of narrative occurs at times in a crime story where, say, dead Uncle Jonathan's journal details, in the novel's first several chapters, some mystifying family event at that time. Then Carole comes across this journal and for the rest of the novel, as a narrating 'I', sets about solving the mystery. She might even, when she uncovers the truth (perhaps in Aunt Isabella's diary, which Uncle Jonathan's finally led her to and which provides yet another first person chapter), decide to conceal this truth from us, the readers. A fourth 'I' comes in then. Detective Superintendent Twist, who, alerted from some little point from Carole, decides to make a few investigations on his own ... and ends up tracking down a mass murderer making out (alliteratively) in Martinique.

THIRD PERSON NARRATOR

Most such stories, however, would employ third person narration. This produces the narrative form written as 'He', 'She' or 'It'. It can range from quite subjective narration, where the narrator is privy to what every character is thinking and feeling, to rather more objective narration, in which the storyteller stays largely outside the characters' consciousnesses and mostly just details what is happening. Completely objective narration would, however, be quite rare.

What third person narration offers is of course a sort of flip side to what has been written above. For example, a third person narrator is not limited to tapping just the one consciousness; but can in fact tap every single consciousness in the novel. What Caesar is feeling, if it is a fiction about Caesar; what Dolly the pop singer is thinking (if anything at all!); even what Fido might be considering reporting to the RSPCA about his unspeakable owners.

You will find examples of third person narration in most books of fiction you will open.

> *Mrs Gardiner's caution to Elizabeth was punctually and*
> *kindly given on the first favourable opportunity of speaking*
> *to her alone; after honestly telling her what she thought,*
> *she thus went on:*

> *"You are too sensible a girl, Lizzy, to fall in love merely*
> *because you are warned against it; and therefore, I am not*
> *afraid of speaking openly ...*

Here, in Jane Austen's PRIDE AND PREJUDICE, you will notice that the author can see directly into Mrs Gardiner's heart — she is feeling "kindly"; and into her head — "honestly".

It is because of this ability to tap the consciousness of every character in a work that a third person narrator is sometimes referred to as an omniscient author. But this advantage carries with it, if not a red light, at least an amber one. To go jumping, over a few pages, from Carole's consciousness to Ron's to D.S Twist's and back to Carole's could have a dispersing effect; whereas you, as author, want rather to hold and concentrate your reader's attention. Jumping around between several consciousnesses does get done; but it's really loading the saddlebags, so to speak.

Third person narration scores well, too, by being able to deal with events and situations anywhere at any time. It is in no way restricted simply to what one narrating 'I' would know nor to where that narrating 'I' happens to be. So in the third person you could have:

> *Meanwhile, across the Straits of Jehoe, Basil flashed a red*
> *alert. Then, his heart full of rage and fear, he swung to*
> *Margo and ...*

Now if you tell this tale with a first person narrator, and this narrator, Carole, is in Sydney when the incident above occurs — how do you, or rather how does Carole, present an account of it to the reader?

> *Basil told me later that across the Straits of Jehoe he*
> *flashed a red alert; then, etc., etc.*

Or:

> *Of course at this time I had no idea that at the very same*
> *moment I was hanging from the Harbour Bridge, Basil had*
> *flashed a red alert from Jehoe, then ...*

Such renderings, however, make it difficult to get anywhere near the heart full of rage and fear, or even to relate the relatively simple swing to Margo.

FURTHER ADVANTAGES OF THIRD PERSON NARRATION

A further opportunity third person narration offers is greater scope for irony.

Dramatic irony, generally speaking, occurs when a reader (or theatre/cinema/television audience) understands rather more about what's actually going on, than do some or all of the fictional characters in the plot; whereas these fictional characters think that *they* are the ones who know it all, and so end up having a rug pulled right out from under them — either comically or tragically, depending on the genre.

So, an unpleasant character gloats loudly over how someone else is due for a real come-uppance over money or social position or a projected marriage. We all know, however, who is to be the very one destined for just such a swatting! In darker mode, King Oedipus in Sophocles' Theban plays, vowed he would do a search-and-destroy for whatever it was that was causing plague in the ancient Greek city of Thebes. He had not the faintest notion that he, himself, was that scourge.

Third person narration increases opportunity, too, for an ironic authorial voice. It is a means by which an author can propose and explore values in a novel; give us an attitude. The opening sentence in PRIDE AND PREJUDICE is an example:

> *It is a truth universally acknowledged, that a single man in*
> *possession of a good fortune, must be in want of a wife.*

What this sentence *seems* to say is that young men with large fortunes devote themselves to searching for wives; whereas what it actually *means*, of course, is that young would-be-wives (or their mothers on their behalf) are out searching for young men with large fortunes! And PRIDE AND PREJUDICE is, as you might expect, to a considerable extent about this situation. The ironic tone persists throughout. It is a way Jane Austen can get herself into the novel, even though the narrative method she's chosen, third person, denies her any sort of direct 'I' presence.

So, the great advantage of third person narration is that you, the author, can tell readers what 'she' thought and what 'he' felt and what 'it' was like. That is, you can occupy any head or heart within the novel, and be any place on earth, and describe to readers what is going on there — even behind locked doors, within sealed cylinders, hidden within a code. You know everything about your story; but your readers do not and neither, in considerable part, do the characters within your story. It will not be until the final pages that your readers, and probably most or all of your characters, will learn whether, despite all the difficulties and hazards, our lovers successfully get together for the long haul. Or whether the crime is foiled or the murderer exposed. Or whether the ambition was achieved; or the planet saved; or ....

Most omniscient authors remain quite anonymous. That is, they don't intrude themselves in any way into their story, don't really concede that they even exist as authors. With the Post Modernism of the past half century or so, though, has come quite a lot of fiction that makes a point of deliberately drawing attention to its 'fictionality' (which is part of what Post Modernism is 'about' taking a stand that fiction is not 'real life').

> She consulted Raphael Faber about the Ph. D. application,
> which went in the same week, the week in which Raphael
> had a long and troubled conversation with Vincent
> Hodgkiss ... *That conversation is not part of the stuff of*
> *this novel, and Frederica was not aware* ... (My italics)

Implicit in this above, from A. S. Byatt's STILL LIFE, is an authorial reminder that this is only a story; the events didn't really happen. Another example would be John Fowles' THE FRENCH LIEUTENANT'S WOMAN, which offers the reader a choice between two endings! (Or for that matter, the character in Shakespeare's TWELFTH NIGHT who remarks, "If this were played upon a stage now, I should condemn it as an improbable fiction" — a tantalising oblique comment suggesting that perhaps we could talk about pre as well as post modernism).

Some interesting novels have been written using certain 'post-mod' techniques, like Elizabeth Jolley's CABIN FEVER and MISS PEABODY'S INHERITANCE; but it is an approach probably best left to the professionals.

Now, finally, a couple of sub-topics.

SETTING AND VIEWPOINT

First, setting. This has some overlap with what the chapter on imagery deals with, but is also strongly linked with narrative as it is the narrator who describes the setting. Obviously, it will not be possible for a narrator to list everything that a scene holds, nor would anyone feel like reading such an enormous inventory. Perec's LIFE: A USER'S MANUAL, must come close to doing so, though; and many find unreadable its pages listing, for example, the contents of every drawer in a cabinet, with the details of every type of screw, and a hardware catalogue reprinted in full!

Hence there must be some selection of items; and of course it is simply common sense to select those particular items that act to suggest, to invoke, the scene as a whole. Take for example:

They reached the highest point in the cemetery, and sat there awhile, gazing out at everything and watching all that was going on.

This gives hardly any sense of place, offers the reader's imagination little from which to build up scene; and probably no one would describe in quite so empty a way. You would go for something rather more like:

They reached the highest point in the cemetery, and sat awhile gazing out over the sweep of tumbled white marble and yellow flowers and the blue Pacific beyond.

Second, viewpoint. This to some extent straddles the whole matter of first and third person narrating. That is, from whose point of view will the story be told? Whose story *is* it?

Sometimes the answers to these two questions is: *No one's in particular.* This is often the case with novels that are family chronicles, covering several generations. The author stays outside every character, just telling us what each is doing. More likely, though, the author will inhabit different characters in turn, perhaps one particular character from each generation; and see events only through that particular pair of eyes. This is more or less what Virginia Woolf does in THE YEARS, some measure of multiple viewpoint.

Much more often, though, you will have one single viewpoint character. With first person narration this viewpoint has necessarily to be that of the narrating 'I'. With third person narration, however, you can choose.

> Though sun still glittered on ocean and sand burned gold
> directly in front of him, Richard felt the day had gone
> suddenly dark. He stared a moment, unseeing, uncertain;
> then making his decision, he turned slowly to Verity.

Richard of course is the viewpoint character here: it's clearly not Verity through whom the story is being told. If it were, though, the passage might go something like this:

> Verity stood with him on the beach. It seemed so lovely to
> her; yet by her side, Richard stood silent, and gloomy. Then
> when he turned slowly, darkly towards her, her heart
> dipped, because she knew this was to be his final decision,
> and that in effect he'd made it for her too.

It is difficult to write of any character without to some extent encompassing that character's viewpoint.

Here's a simple example, from a 1950's crime story selected quite randomly from whatever was to hand. The central character is the private investigator and "baggage" Eve Gill, and the narration is in the first person. Read every sentence carefully and take note of the specific first person narration qualities there.

> Those wide and desolate marshes, the flat grey-green sea
> beyond, the big sky, all this was my world, familiar from
> my earliest memories. I had been born in that house to
> which we were returning, its tall chimneys twisting higher
> than the trees which sheltered it. Ten generations of Gills
> had lived there and I was of their blood and this corner of

the earth was my heritage and a solid anchorage for my heart.

I stole a look at Christopher's face — that gloomy disillusion in it — that must be driven out with all the courage I could muster. He must be kept aware of me, physically, sensually aware of me. All the time. This was Saturday, and not yet noon. I had until Monday — call it Sunday night, since he would have to catch the early train back to London on Monday morning. Even so it was a lifetime of opportunity. If I couldn't re-establish this thing between us by then I deserved to lose him.

PERSPECTIVES

One other aspect of point of view picks up what Kate Grenville states in the quotation heading this chapter. This is that all fiction is written from some perspective on the part of the author, either deliberately assumed or just intrinsically there. Jane Austen, for example, recognised that she was writing from a woman's viewpoint, so never attempted to represent a man *from within*, only ever as he would appear in company. Likewise, an Australian Aboriginal writer like Sally Morgan would probably choose to make her Aboriginal perspective clear in her works. Many writers, of course, adopt a fictional persona if they want to write from the perspective of the opposite sex, or of someone from another culture or period of time. This carries certain hazards to do with feasibility; but it can be done and often is.

Many writers indicate their particular perspectives from the beginning. It might be by choice of subject, or by tone. David Lodge, for example, writes SMALL WORLD from an academic's perspective.

"When April with its sweet showers has pierced the drought of March to the root"...as the poet Geoffrey Chaucer observed many years ago, folk long to go on pilgrimages. Only these days, professional people call them conferences.

The advantage of a writer understanding the point of view from which he/she is writing is that it gives very clear signals and directions to the reader as to what sort of novel is coming up. And if this reader knows this, even if there are unknowns ahead in it as, say, some mystery to be solved, then this same reader can feel confident that the author knows what he/she is doing, and adjust his/her reader approach to it. If you signal crime novel or family chronicle, and your work turns out to be Celtic fantasy or plain farce, you'll likely leave your reader stranded the other side of a considerable expectation-gap.

One last word, for any oppressed at the prospect of having to weigh up all the this-that-and-the-other about narration before getting a word of a planned novel down on paper. Not so! You can expect that to a considerable extent the narrative, viewpoint and perspective decisions will pretty much make themselves for you. Stories seem to present with these already part of the package. This will be particularly so as you become a more experienced writer. Your unconscious does the sorting and programming for you, before you begin and as you go along.

Understanding these matters about narration, however, enables you more effectively to exploit the advantages of whatever narrative mode you are working in, and to avoid or minimise the restrictions that might come with it. And knowing exactly what you are doing can prove wonderfully comforting and helpful when you hit a bump, find some difficulty with a script, and your instincts fail or get momently confused. To be able to fetch some informed analysis to both creating and editing problems, is like having some nursing skills when the kids suddenly report sick or injured, or mechanical know-how when the stupid car won't start!

9

Structure

At present, nothing is talked of, nothing admired, but what
I cannot help calling a very insipid and tedious
performance: it is a kind of novel, called THE LIFE AND
OPINIONS OF TRISTRAM SHANDY; the great
humour of which consists in the whole narration always
going backwards.

HORACE WALPOLE (1717-79)

When the great Irish poet William Butler Yeats asked in
"A Prayer for my Daughter": *"How can you tell the
dancer from the dance?"*, he had a perceptive
question! Neither *dance* nor *dancer* can exist in isolation one
from the other. You need a *dancer*, to have a *dance* going; and
you need some actual *dancing* before you can have a *dancer*
there. It is much the same with structure (or form) and content
(or matter) in literary works. We can discuss each separately; but
they cannot *exist* separately, in isolation. Structure must be the
structure of something.

With fiction, the main structuring components would
probably be plot and theme, though character, and setting, and
imagery and other such, can have structural significance too.

But to the practical: how do you best organise and order all
the components and the material of your novel? That is, how do
you structure?

The question sounds a somewhat daunting one; but
fortunately the answer is reassuringly simple and straightforward.

For one thing, you'll structure around time. You will almost certainly have a Time Line, either basically chronological, as it mostly is with Dickens and Jane Austen for example, or with some specific and significant reordering of events along this Time Line, as with WUTHERING HEIGHTS.

DRAMATIC RHYTHM

Beyond that, you will in most cases organise your narrative material into a dramatic rhythm. That is, you will devise a series of episodes, each with its own beginning and end; with tempo rising as each episode follows the other; with a series of crises overlaying these that culminate in a 'climax' and then 'resolution'. Somewhat thus:

In Jane Austen's PRIDE AND PREJUDICE, (a novel, to put it crudely, about the "marriage market"), two sisters, Jane and Elizabeth, meet two young men, Bingley and Darcy, much wealthier than they are and in a higher social bracket. Jane and Bingley fall in love. Elizabeth and Darcy appear not to like each other at all; kept apart, the reader comes to realise, by pride and prejudice. Principally, *his* pride and *her* prejudice. Darcy's pride even affects Bingley's romance as Darcy, persuading himself that Jane is not really serious about Bingley and detesting the vulgarity of her family, in turn persuades his modest friend that he is mistaken about Jane's affection for him.

The story is really Elizabeth and Darcy's; indeed mainly Elizabeth's, as it charts her growth to self-knowledge and to an understanding of her prejudiced blindness to Darcy's true nature (the climax point); which leads to the admission of her love for him. He, in his turn, long knowing he loves Elizabeth, but out of pride fighting this love, eventually learns *his* lesson: "...dearest, loveliest Elizabeth! What do I not owe you! You taught me a lesson, hard indeed at first ..." (the resolution). There have been lots of other problems on the way, all sorted out as part of this resolution. Elizabeth and Darcy marry, of course. So, too, do Jane and Bingley, Darcy having made a clean breast to his friend of his part in their separation.

Most novels, stories, narrative poetry, plays, movies and tele-serials follow this 'dramatic' rhythm, or some modification of it; though throughout this century a number of authors have attempted to eschew it altogether or at least to disguise it. It is fascinating that this particular rhythm is one we're already very familiar with from other areas of experience — a sort of growth-leading-to-climax-and-ending-with-cease paradigm:

WAVES begin, build up slowly, CRASH DOWN, and dissipate.

STORMS announce themselves with sultriness, build up darkly, CRASH ABOVE, then sunshine again.

THE YEAR is born with Spring, flourishes as Summer, POURS FORTH HARVEST, then disperses into Winter.

DAY wakes at Dawn, climbs through Morning, BLAZES HIGH NOON, then descends through Afternoon into Night.

SEXUAL ENCOUNTER opens with glances, proceeds through foreplay to tumescence to congress, EXPLODES TO CLIMAX, relaxes to post-coital tristesse (or cream-bun smile!)

The CAREER kicks off as office boy/tea girl, proceeds to salesperson, then branch manager, then perhaps to COMPANY DIRECTOR, to ebb in due course into retirement and the superannuation package.

It is perhaps because this dramatic rhythm so permeates our experiences, that we find it such a natural and satisfying a skeleton for so much of our literature.

ROUND AND ROUND IN CIRCLES

Another structure used for fiction, particularly for plays in the Theatre of the Absurd, is that of the flat circle. Here, events do not escalate to climax, then resolve and conclude. Quite the opposite; the events more likely circle, without any increase in tensions, back to where they began, without, often, any sense of finish at all, of completion. There will probably have been no progress from the starting point; nothing resolved; all set to repeat much the same circle again. Samuel Beckett's play WAITING FOR GODOT is one such. Each act ends with:

"Let's go."
"We can't."
"Why not?"
"We're waiting for Godot."

If there were fifty acts to this play, each would return to, and conclude with, that withdrawal from action, into waiting.

It is unlikely you'll want to structure your fiction strictly on this kind of circular pattern, because by its very nature it's short on the dramatic and hence difficult to make compelling reading or watching. A variation of it, as the theme 'The wheel has turned full circle' is, however, a common enough one, and an effective one too. Such a circularity is achieved in an interesting and innovative manner in Shirley McLaughlin's recently published BILLY BATCHELOR. She uses, in a way, two openings. The first is actually Preface:

> There are few visitors any more. People get tired of sickness. Of late, those who do drop in have taken to telling me all about their lives, how much trouble they've seen, how tough the world is today, how lucky I am to be out of it!
>
> I listen. I counsel too. Why not? I have nothing better to do. Sometimes I laugh, unkindly I suppose, watch the dream as it breaks in the widened pupils of their eyes. Wish I could catch those short glimpses, little bits of future as they dawn ... wish I could gather them up, put them back into my eyes, my heart. But to no avail.
>
> It's too late for me.
>
> Yet I had it all once.

This, of course, is actually a conclusion, that point-of-looking-back to which the novel will eventually fetch you.

Shirley McLaughlin's Chapter 1, which (naturally) immediately follows the Preface, swings right back to the beginning of it all; that is, to Billy's birth:

> I was born in a condemned house in Kurra Kurra on 4 July 1914.
>
> On arrival into this world, I sneezed, and did little else, so I've been told, for the next sixty hours. All three and a half pounds of me was wrapped in a grey army blanket and placed in a chipped green enamel bath, along with five other new people, each of whom was apparently of normal weight, looks and behaviour. Much can be read into such comment, but I took it to mean that I was but a weak pittance worth, particularly ugly and totally incapable of sensible baby antics, like crying.

Were it not for that looking-back-Preface, there'd be little in this opening (besides the author's lively prose) to impel a reader forward. But with the Preface, there are curiosities to be satisfied, aroused partly by the very fact that *the wheel has come full circle* for that tiny, sneezing baby. What happened to bring about that sad conclusion; all that disillusion? Why is it now "too late"? "too late" for what? Yet Billy's prose, as she begins her story, is vigorous, controlled, self-aware, good humoured, certainly without any sense of the born loser. So we'd better read on!

PARABOLA

Another rhythm underlying structure is that of the parabola. Here, the events might be seen to start at a certain point on a line, swing out from that point ... and then back to the line again. But, not to that same point they launched from. Rather, further along the line, thus:

Frederica, in A.S. Byatt's THE VIRGIN IN THE GARDEN, is red-haired, freckled and academically brilliant in her final school year, and breaking her neck for a scholarship to university, in part so she can leave home. This is her position at both the beginning and the end of the novel. In between, all sorts of deeply emotional and disruptive things happen to her parents and to her brother and sister, although these leave Frederica almost untouched. However, in a play-cum-pageant, the virgin in the garden of the title, she plays the young Queen Elizabeth. She has to learn to *act* the part of a sexually precocious young woman who is chased around the garden but who successfully eludes her pursuers. Soon after, she finds herself forced, in real life and again successfully — to 'act' the same scenario in the big house overnight! Then she deliberately and rather theatrically loses her virginity with a young man who can only say afterwards: "All that blood!" The parabola-like structure thus brings Frederica to the end of the novel, being offered two scholarships. Though she remains in something of the same position as when she started, because of her experiences in the interval she is actually much further along the line in terms of emotional maturity.

What occurs then during this parabolic swing out — often from our familiar world to some simpler world where things are seen more clearly — is that experiences sort things out. Learning, or realisations, occur; and these fresh insights, these new orderings, are fetched back to the familiar world, and incorporated into it. Which is why the point returned to is further along the line than the point departed from.

This structure is seen very clearly in many of Shakespeare's plays. In AS YOU LIKE IT the characters move from a brutal Court ... to the Forest of Arden, where all the love relationships get sorted out and the Court world "cleansed" ... then back to the reconstituted Court again. In A MIDSUMMER NIGHT'S DREAM, something of the same happens, though this time the 'parabolic journey' is from a Court into a wood outside Athens and back, and both the erotic and social aspects of love relationships are encountered. In THE MERCHANT OF VENICE there is some similar movement between the Venice of Antonio and Shylock, and Portia's Belmont, though the parabola here isn't quite so straightforward.

If you discount the final page of THE CATCHER IN THE RYE, you have Holden Caulfield moving out from the familiar world of 1960s USA (i.e. Pency School) to the simpler role of Wanderer in New York and then back to 1960s USA again as, through Phoebe, he reconciles himself to growing up. There's perhaps a parabola underlying WUTHERING HEIGHTS too — indeed, two, if you see the narrator Lockwood moving from his familiar world to the more elemental world of Heathcliff; then, a sadder and a wiser man perhaps, back to his former 'civilised' and urban world. There is also the rhythm of Heathcliff himself swinging out from the slum child who is nothing, through all the experiences of The Heights and The Grange ... back to nothing again, in the graveyard this time.

THE INTRUDER

Another structure is that of the disrupting intruder. With this, you have a settled situation — a family, a firm, a community, a relationship — and someone or something comes in from outside, challenging and threatening, and so inevitably destabilising and disordering. Pearl Fulton does just this in "Bliss". Johnno fulfils something of the role in the Malouf work: he is the maverick outside force that the narrator Dante spends a whole novel attempting to accommodate. The wild, dark little slum child that Mr Earnshaw fetches in to "Wuthering Heights", is certainly another 'intruder' acting as destructive catalyst. So is Peter Walsh, returning from India and from Clarissa Dalloway's past, in Virginia Woolf's MRS DALLOWAY.

JOURNEYING

Finally, there is a complex of related structures which might be seen as owing a deal to the epic; the classical epic, not the contemporary blockbuster kind. In works like Homer's ULYSSES and Virgil's AENEID, the hero's journey consists of a series of episodes which, while they do have a movement from a beginning to a general conclusion, are also largely self-contained, each one something of a complete story on its own. This episodic form was used by eighteenth writers like Henry Fielding, who in JOSEPH ANDREWS has several individuals and groups travelling from London to Bath, criss-crossing and meeting up in a seemingly random manner, experiencing self-contained comic adventures. Tobias Smollett, with rough-hewn tales like HUMPHREY CLINKER, PEREGRINE PICKLE and RODERICK RANDOM, is another. These were known as picaresque novels. Nearer our own time is Jerome K. Jerome's THREE MEN IN A BOAT; and nearer again that 1970s cult novel, Robert Pirsig's ZEN AND THE ART OF MOTOR CYCLE MAINTENANCE. The road movie, and even tele-series like YES MINISTER and THE BILL, probably have some kinship.

MULTIPLE STRUCTURES

It will be apparent that some novels might be seen to contain many differing structures, depending on the way you approach them. Indeed, several have already been indicated for WUTHERING HEIGHTS; and yet these in no way exhaust discernible structures there. The novel could additionally be seen as a fictionalised biography of Heathcliff. If you reorganise its Time Line into the actual chronology of the events themselves, you have these events beginning with the arrival of Heathcliff at "Wuthering Heights" and ending with Heathcliff's death there. (The work couldn't start with Heathcliff's birth and infancy, as those are quite unknown.) Certainly this is the biographical way Nelly sees her story. She calls it, "the history of Mr Heathcliff".

WUTHERING HEIGHTS has even been seen as having a Marxist structure! Heathcliff represents the dispossessed masses — no wealth, no property, no education, no social status, no 'family'. He responds, according to the critic Arnold Kettle, simply by getting these class weapons of education and wealth and the law; and by using arranged marriages and the like against both the Lintons and Earnshaws — "the classic methods of the ruling class, expropriation and property deals".

> He buys out Hindley and reduces him to drunken
> impotency. He marries Isabella then organises the
> marriage of their son to Catherine Linton, so that the entire
> property of the two families shall be controlled by himself.
> He systematically degrades Hareton Earnshaw to servility.
> "I want the triumph of seeing MY descendants fairly lord of
> THEIR estates! My child hiring their children to till their
> father's lands for wages."

Such a Marxist account of structure certainly fits Bronte's novel, (though of course it leaves out a great deal too). Which makes it rather interesting that one of the best politico-economic novels of the nineteenth century was written under the very same Yorkshire roof. Charlotte Bronte's SHIRLEY deals with industrial relations and riots in the cotton milling areas of northern England. It is additionally intriguing to realise that at much the same time Emily was creating WUTHERING HEIGHTS, not so very far away Karl Marx was hammering out DAS KAPITAL!

By this point, two things will probably have become obvious to you. The first is that there are really many structure paradigms and that the examples so far are for the most part of the more common. But quite unusual structures can be found, as with Henry Fielding's rollicking TOM JONES, one of the very first novels ever. Its chapters are arranged "architecturally", so that the first third (precisely) of the novel can be seen as a column; the second third as an arch with one end resting on that column; and the final third as the other supporting column. Right where the keystone of this arch would be — that is, where in architecture all the competing stresses would meet and intersect — is a chapter in which almost all the main characters also meet and intersect, at a particular country inn; though not all are aware of the others' presence. The eighteenth century loved these sorts of architectural correspondences and symmetries, which appear in music and poetry of the age too.

The second thing is that often a novel will have two or more structures operating simultaneously, different approaches revealing different patterns of ordering, though in almost all cases, the dramatic rhythm will be there too. WUTHERING HEIGHTS certainly has the gradually rising tempo, with crises, and so on; but if you see it that Cathy and Heathcliff are reunited finally and that as spirits they wander the moors together again, then you've something of the full circle structure; because that's how their relationship began, wandering the moors together, free and in amity.

CHAPTERS

Whatever your overriding structure, you will almost certainly want to break up your total mass of material into smaller, more manageable units. It may seem odd not to provide a chapter specifically *on* chapters; but so much of the matter relevant to that topic is covered under other heads.

Essentially, though, chapters are useful as breakpoints in your ongoing narrative. Chapters usually have their own inner structures, of course, in that they have to build a point to a particular height of interest. They grow and develop in something of the way the novel as a whole does; without necessarily having to resolve crises or bring action to any finality. Rather, because their function is to contribute to the continuing action of the work overall, the end of a chapter will leave a particular action incomplete, with the reader in (one trusts!) some measure of suspense. Even if a particular action in the chapter is itself completed, the reader is left wondering how, where, when and for what reason, this is going to affect the overall story and its characters. In his ART OF FICTION David Lodge says:

> "... *chapter breaks are useful for marking transitions*
> *between different times or places in the action ...Thackeray*
> *uses the concluding line of a chapter like the curtain line of*
> *a play, to heighten an effect of surprise and suspense.*
> *Beginning a new chapter can also have a useful expressive*
> *or rhetorical effect, especially if it has a textual heading.*

Smollett's chapter-headings, for instance, are like film
trailers, enticing the reader with the promise of exciting
action."

George Eliot uses chapter headings which read something
like a skeletal plan for the progress of the action. Her long novel,
ADAM BEDE, like much Victorian fiction, is divided into three
volumes, each containing two 'Books', which in their turn are
subdivided into chapters. The novel's climax occurs in Book Fifth
(Vol. 3) and the resolution takes up the sixth and final book. The
action of the fifth book concerns the young girl Hetty's running
away from home, fruitlessly seeking Arthur, her lover; leaving her
new-born and illegitimate child in a forest to die; being
discovered, tried for murder, and sentenced. Here are the chapter
headings, which give some feeling of the author's treatment of
the issue:

BOOK FIFTH

36. The Journey in Hope

37. The Journey in Despair

38. The Quest

39. The Tidings

40. The Bitter Waters Spread

41. The Eve of the Trial

42. The Morning of the Trial

43. The Verdict

44. Arthur's Return

45. In the Prison

46. The Hours of Suspense

47. The Last Moment

48. Another Meeting in the Wood

Not all novels give titles to their chapters. But E. Annie
Proulx's Pulitzer Prize winning, THE SHIPPING NEWS, does (see
overleaf).

Quoyle is the main character of this novel and the chapter
headings direct us to aspects of his character and his story. Hence
this and the other headings are thematic. They also play on the
'shipping' associations of the title as you'll realise.

1

Quoyle

Quoyle: A coil of rope.

*"A Flemish flake is a spiral coil of one layer only.
It is made on deck, so that it may be
walked on if necessary."*

THE ASHLEY BOOK OF KNOTS

Here is an account of a few years in the life of Quoyle, born in Brooklyn
and raised in a shuffle of dreary upstate towns.

2. Love Knot   (This heading builds on the notion of
knots, and is not only thematic, it also
contributes to plot and action.)

3. Strangle Knot   (You guess what happens here?)

4. Cast Away   ("Cast Away, to be forced from a ship by a
disaster." THE MARINER'S DICTIONARY.)

So it goes on.

SECTIONS

Some authors divide their work into numbered but unnamed chapters. Quite often an author using chapters will also divide the work into named sections. Drusilla Modjeska, a contemporary Australian writer, follows this practice in THE ORCHARD. She is obviously using these sections to indicate something important about structure, and the Contents page reads as follows:

In his famous A PASSAGE TO INDIA, a novel about the British Raj which filmed particularly well, E.M. Forster's Contents page reads:

When you know the novel, you realise that these sections divide the action in terms of plot, and also of time; but that the headings are obviously also thematic, pinpointing most skilfully the central issues within the narrative.

REASSURANCES

By way of conclusion — two reassurances.

The first is that while you will readily be able to abstract basic structure, or structures, from any work of fiction, you will frequently find that the skeleton(s) you abstract often don't precisely fit any forms outlined here. Sometimes, for example, a dramatic rhythm might feature a very rapid rising action, with the climax occurring mid-work or even earlier; then a long drawn out falling action. Shakespeare's MACBETH and JULIUS CAESAR each fit this somewhat, if you consider the assassinations of King Duncan and Julius Caesar as the respective climaxes — the first occurs in the second of five acts; the second, at the beginning of the third act. After that, a quite lengthy series of consequences of those assassinations are traced, with Macbeth's execution and Brutus' suicide coming in each play's final moments.

The second reassurance is this — that if writing a novel depended on one having it all in one's head to begin with, and then starting with sentence one of Chapter I and writing it right through from there to THE END, not all that many novels might end up getting written!

While it is likely that at some point in your work you will suddenly take off, and begin writing it as a running narrative in chapter order, like telling a story, it is rather less likely that you'll be able to launch your novel in so dashing a way. Many a piece which could reasonably be considered half-finished, might still consist of heaps of fragments in its author's folders — scenes, character sketches, incidents and ideas for incidents, several possible beginnings or endings, some research notes on Celtic Wales or plastics manufacture or slow-acting poisons, some passages of dialogue or of interior debate, some phrases to be incorporated, some half chapters and tentative listing of chapters and chapter heads and suggestions for chapter ordering — and a deal more!

At such a point you could well be looking for all that folder material to start to come together, feeling that you do have a novel, fragmented and disordered and rough as it might be. Patience thenceforward is all; and there can be great satisfaction in realising that you don't have actually to write very much more, just get to work on what you've already produced, watch it take shape and blossom under your ministrations. Well, that's what we all hope!

Structuring, then, like so much about writing, is more to be 'absorbed' than 'learned'. But, again like much about writing, it is empowering to be able to understand what it is you are in fact absorbing, and so be in a position to see what it is that is happening when something in your work turns all ornery and be-like-that-then. And the way to enlightenment about structuring is, for the third time like so much about writing, to check out other fiction, and see how these other writers are ordering, shaping, their material.

10

Editing & Revision

Verbum semel emissum volat irrevocabile.
A word once uttered flies off irrevocably.

HORACE

Happily, the Roman poet's dictum does not apply to words 'uttered' per typewriter or computer screen! Most writers are, in fact, 'revoking' much of the time as they work along, as well as after they finish each draft. They keep casting back over preceding sentences, paragraphs, pages; they continuingly add, delete, reorder, rephrase. Indeed, not even final publication will necessarily bring editing and revising to an end, in that some writers will give their piece another work-over for a second edition. STATUES AGAINST THE SKY, a section of which will be quoted shortly, went 'through the machine' at least two dozen times!

There is unfortunately, though, not a great deal about editing and revising that can be taught. It's more a feeling for how a piece reads and how it might be improved. This comes from that heightened sensibility some folk have naturally, and others gain from experience. Writers who can sense what is not working in a passage, and what is, are fortunate indeed; particularly if they can respond so to their own work. Other writers just go into free-fall when it comes to assessing what they've written; and if this is your experience, you'll need to get someone to co-operate with you on revision and editing. If you're profitable enough, an editor or agent will do it for you. Otherwise, you have a problem;

because relatives and friends are usually not competent for such a task, and anyway would probably prove more anxious to please and reassure than actually to help!

Very occasionally, there are authors who write splendidly first up and so never need to revise and edit. Charles Hamilton was one such; and as he probably published more fiction in English than anyone else in the history of the universe, he will have saved himself much editing! Hamilton is probably best remembered now for his schoolboy stories earlier this century, the fat Billy Bunter being his most popular character. He typed on coloured paper, which went straight into a coloured envelope and off to his (delighted) publisher.

Here, however, are a few suggestions to help with revising and editing.

When writing, use the margins of your typed or printed sheet to note anything occurring to you about possible revisions later. Even a question mark beside a passage will remind that you're not entirely satisfied at that point; and would probably be better than breaking into the flow of your writing in an attempt to resolve some misgiving on the spot. Later, you might decide that there is in fact no problem there, so you just leave as-is. Or you spot the problem and address it. In the same way, if while you're writing you use a word or phrase that you're doubtful about, circle it for attention later. Jot in the margin, too, any alternatives that present. Even plot alternatives. *What if Dexter phoned Sibby and told her the truth??* These might prove of great value, if later your novel gets bogged down.

If when you go back to a passage marked for further attention, you find that you're still uncertain, still unable to sort the passage out, try dropping it altogether. It's surprising how often such an intractable slab will not be missed, indeed, that the work will read better without it. There is an example of this try-it-without-it ploy later in this chapter.

If a scene reads flat, have you 'milked' it for all it's worth? Checking this out will involve you in considerations of characterisation, of setting, of plot and structure, of theme, of imagery, of dialogue; and most of all, of the dramatic generally. Have you brought out the action, the tensions, the emotion?

Look back at the confrontation between Caroline Bell and Clive Leadbetter in Chapter 6 on dialogue. Superficially, this is just a conflict over a woman's objection to having to prepare lunches for the male staff. Shirley Hazzard gets real flashpoint from it — sharply realised characters who are opposed to each other in almost every possible way. An allegedly trivial disagreement explodes to a quite substantial gender issue; to dialogue that's like a volleyball being smashed back from one to the other; and of course to significant plot movement. Every dramatic possibility the initial situation offers, would seem to have been exploited.

Note that there appears to be scarcely one superfluous word in this Caroline Bell scene — which indicates another revision procedure — editing back. In first draft writing, many words present on the page often aren't at all necessary. It is surprising how many words can be cut from passages, with better writing emerging! As freelancers needing to wring every honest dollar from our work (we did have four littlies to clothe, shelter and feed!), we learned that stories placed in England at 3,000 words could then be reduced to 1,300 for a North American weekly, and to 1,000 for an Education Department magazine here in Australia. A few of these stories were additionally 'tailored' for radio, or for New Zealand publications!

The work of no two writers will offer quite the same cutting-back opportunities. One promising area to tackle, though, would be those descriptive passages. Phrases and images often duplicate one another. *The cold wind froze him to his bones.* Why *cold* here? Surely *froze* does that job? You will often find, too, that some scenes or episodes can be dropped out altogether, in that they are either repetitious, or not essentially part of the story, of either its plot or its theme. The try-it-without-it ploy again.

As a final cutting-back check, go through your work with the several fiction-components heads in mind: plot, characterisation, imagery and the like. Look at each episode, and at each incident within each episode. Is it part of your plot? Does it spell out, or is it at least consistent with, your theme? Sometimes fragments that were relevant at first have become no longer so, because as your novel went on you made changes elsewhere. Be fairly ruthless. You are more likely to weaken your work by leaving in than by tipping out.

It is difficult to give examples of revision and editing, because for the most part we don't have any of the original manuscripts for works in print; so we can't sight what the pages in front of us were changed from. To read in the British Library though, the first versions of Virginia Woolf's MRS DALLOWAY, was to confirm for us the impression that much of the imagery in the published work has a sexual, erotic basis, it was more explicitly so in the manuscript, and had been 'toned back' for the version finally published.

EXAMPLE

For a less exalted example of editing and revising, we make do with a short story "Tiring the Sun" in STATUES AGAINST THE SKY about two lovers wandering a cemetery and finding that all the *memento mori* there throws their love relationship into a rather longer perspective. Very much a mood-theme story; with the resolution, simply a redirection of attitude. Here is an extract from an early version.

> They wandered then along grassy tracks. Collapsed graves spilled the hot of pigface and thrust out spikes of salty sword-plant. There was the detritus of abandoned homage — broken jars; rusted wire frames that had held bouquets; headstones with leaden letters dropped away or golden names weathering some beloved into eternal anonymity. They spoke little, though each was sunning in the awareness that the other was only a hand touch away.
>
> The Memorial, a marble wall enclosing a court the size of a large room, had two bronze hounds sentinel at its entrance; and within, also bronze, reliefs of alarums and excursions. Carmel read out:
>
> > Who fears to speak of Ninety Eight?
> > Who blushes at the name?
> > When cowards mock the patriots' fate,
> > Who hangs his head for shame?
>
> "Goodness," she murmured. "Who indeed?"
>
> "When I ran snotty-nosed and barefoot," he told her, "I used to spy on the gatherings here. Every whenever. From some finely judged middle-distance, of course — they were a

fierce lot, they'd get after you with full Cuchulain howls. Havin' after the little cheeky .... — something like that. " He added: "No one seems to rage here now, half a century on. But it mattered then, those Irish passions. But not now. Not here anyway."

"I half understand you." She laughed. "I AM half Irish!"

He took her arm.

"I'll show you a very particular death, while you're here."

He led her ...

In the revised version, you will note both addition and (and rather more) cutting. The most substantial change was the dropping of the paragraph beginning "When I ran ..." It was seen as really extraneous to both plot and theme; though as it was so redolent of a childhood experience, it was yielded up most reluctantly! It seems not in the least missed though? Salutary?

They wandered in comfortable silence then, down grassy aisles. Collapsed graves spilled the pink of pig-face and thrust out spikes of salty sword-plant. There was the detritus of abandoned obsequy — broken jars, rusted flower frames, headstones with letters missing now and weathering into anonymity some confidently-proclaimed beloved.

Each sunned in the awareness that the other was a mere hand-touch away.

The Memorial, a marble wall with a gate of black iron pickets, enclosed a court the size of a very large room. It had two bronze hounds sentinel; and within, also bronze, dramatic reliefs of Irish alarums and assassinations. Beneath were, allegedly, the remnants of Michael Dwyer, THE WICKLOW CHIEF, and his wife Mary.

Carmel hoisted herself, hung precariously, read out —

Who fears to speak of Ninety Eight —
Who blushes at the name?
When cowards mock the patriots' fate,
Who hangs his head in shame?

"Goodness!" She smiled winningly downwards. "Who indeed!"

"They mattered then, those Irish passions." And, after some pause — "It still matters that it mattered then."

"I half understand you." She permitted his hands to accept her small waist; dropped. "Well — I am half Irish."

"I'll present you a more particular death. While you're here."

He led this time ...

There comes a stage when you'll feel you've done about all the editing and revising you can see to do. It is a good idea to put the manuscript away for a time then, while you work on something else. Later, when you've quite forgotten that first document, you come back to it, see it all relatively freshly. These sorts of revisings can keep recurring, sandwiched between other works, until you decide you've done about as well with the initial piece as you are able to do, or until the work has for some reason, like a publisher's deadline or the strictures of topicality, to head out into the world and take its chance whatever.

Keep, for a time, all those pages-with-cuts, as occasionally rejected scraps can be used elsewhere; or even reinstated, should you change your mind about them.

Malcolm Lowry remarked once that the most effective way to improve one's manuscript was to select all the very best passages in it... and throw them out! This is perhaps drastic; but apprentice writers in particular are notorious for 'purple passages'. Indeed, when Malcolm Lowry sent to Conrad Aiken the manuscript of his early novel (ULTRAMARINE) about a ship's voyage through the Straits of Magellan, that experienced author suggested (twinklingly?) the work's title be changed to PURPLE PASSAGE!

RUDIMENTS OF WRITING

Finally, something about the more formal elements associated with editing; like spelling, punctuation, and grammar generally.

This section can be considered optional, as many of you will require little or no guidance here. Experience with creative writing schools and courses, however, has shown that a great many apprentice writers do look for help with managing such formal elements; and that many of these in turn find it useful and of interest to understand something of the reasonings and history behind accepted usage. So....

Spelling

There are no really correct spellings, only 'accepted' spellings. English is the product of a number of languages and dialects as well as changes over time. Words drifting in over centuries, were spelled much as they sounded at the time to those borrowing the words, rather than as they were spelled by those from whom they were borrowed — as with the French rendering Old English *cwen* as *queen*. And along with William the Conquerer came, almost certainly, the Old French *boef, porc, moton*; which have become the English *beef, pork* and *mutton*. Records of the early Middle Ages show a dozen different ways of spelling *might!*

Even script features influenced spellings. Because the letters *m, n, u, v,* and *w* were written very similarly, making some words hard to read in script, *u* would sometimes be replaced by *o*; which is why *luv* and *cum* are spelt *love* and *come*.

Towards the end of this early period though, several factors pushed towards some standardisation of spelling. There was a great expansion of government records and in the employment for these of the Royal Chancery Standard, from France; the rise of literature in English (like Chaucer's THE CANTERBURY TALES); and of course the invention of printing. A couple of centuries later again, dictionaries began; and then the move towards universal education.

Spelling, which had once been pretty much optional, became increasingly prescriptive. Indeed, one of the ways in which people today will assess your social class and your standards of education and literacy generally, will be your spelling. It's a tyranny; but if you want the respect of editors and colleagues; if you are to avoid the risk of a 'bad impression' prejudicing assessment of your work; you will need to keep your spelling 'correct'. A dictionary is probably the best resource, even though this method depends on your knowing which words you need to look up, and also being familiar enough with a word's possible spellings to be able to find it in the first place! These days, too, many writers will have computers with spelling check facilities.

Watch out for American spellings though; these are strongly contra-indicated with some editors.

Some spelling problems are really *wrong word* problems, like *two/too/to*. This particular confusion is quite readily sorted out. *two* is the number 2; *too* means *also, as well;* and any other use is *to*. So, "I'll go *to* the movies and my *two* brothers will come *too*."

Other groups of homonyms that trip you up, you just have to set out and learn. It's not difficult. For example: *bare* skin; and grizzly *bear*, *bear* pain.

Grammar

Grammar is, like spelling, something of a blundering about. Because English is basically a Germanic language, and the grammar imposed on it largely Latinate, the fit isn't always a comfortable one. This renders some rules of grammar neither very practical nor easy to follow. (Instances of this will be dealt with later in the chapter.)

There is much difference of opinion as to whether learning grammar will actually guide you into writing better English. For example, ponder this situation with what are known as Adjective Zones:

That same old green Australian history book.

Adjectives in such a phrase tend to follow a quite definite ordering rule. Closest to the noun *book* come any adjectives that are really nouns — like *history* but are being used in an adjectival way. Then come adjectives that are 'close to' being nouns — like *Australian*, which is almost *Australia*. Next, colour adjectives — here, *green*. Finally, any other adjectives, as *old*. There occurs a somewhat similar ordering in: *any recent brown Holden car manual*.

Now, you almost certainly don't realise that you already know these rules for ordering adjectives in a phrase. But you do! Otherwise, you'd be writing/saying: *that same history green Australian old book!* and *any brown car Holden recent manual*. And you didn't learn about Adjective Zones from any grammar text? You picked it up simply from usage.

Notwithstanding the above, a simple book on traditional grammar could be useful, dealing with the few main anxieties writers tend to suffer. If you add to this something on functional grammar, you'll be helping yourself to fascinating insights into how our language works under the bonnet, as it were.

Here are a few usages which seem to give some writers anxiety.

Apostrophes

First, that baffling apostrophe. *It's* or *its? Whose* or *who's? The boy's book* or *the boys' book? There* or *their* or *they're?*

Apostrophes usually represent a letter or letters dropped. In *It's Saturday, It's* is a contraction of *it is*. The *i* has been dropped from *It is*, so an apostrophe is there in its place: *It's*. It's (!) the same with *Today's Saturday* and *Ron's coming soon (Today is* and *Ron is)*.

But with: *the dog ate its dinner*, *'its'* is not a contraction for *it is*. *The dog ate it is dinner* makes no sense. There has been no *i* dropped. Hence, no apostrophe.

Similarly with: *The firm announced its plans* and *its regulator, the technician explained ...*

This explanation — the apostrophe replacing a missing letter (or letters) — applies with all the following:

The Maori WHOSE book was published.
WHO'S the Maori whose book was published? (Who is)

YOUR manuscript was lost in the post.
YOU'RE the author whose manuscript ... (You are)

THERE were several young men. (There is, there seem, there have been, there might ...)
THERE, beside the stove. (Place)
THEIR bookcase is full. (Possession)
THEY'RE very upset. (They are)

Here are some others:

Isn't = is not	Weren't = were not
Could've = could have	Can't = cannot
Hasn't = has not	We'll = we will
She'd = she would.	Let's = let us
Fred's = Fred is.	We're = we are.

The apostrophe indicating ownership, possession, is quite another matter and a little more tricky; but it would seem in most instances to be replacing a letter too — the letter *e*. In the

Germanic Old English, where Modern English has its origins, possession was shown in most one-owner instances by adding *es* to the end of the possessor, the owning, word. So, with the OE word for *king* being *cyning*, if the king had a ship, the phrase would be *cyninges scipe* — *the king's ship*. If this practice had lasted through to Modern English, though, we'd have it as *the kinges ship*. Or *the boyes leg*. Or *the womanes husband*. One might assume that the *e* dropped out for speech reasons — well, who wants to say *boy-es* and *king-es* and *woman-es?* The apostrophe seems to have come in to replace the *e* dropped in the actual saying of each word — *the king's ship, the boy's leg, the woman's husband.*

What about *boys'* and the like, though? That is, the apostrophe following the *s?*

Proceed thus:

Write down the possessor (owner) word. In our example above there was only the one boy; but if we were talking about the legs of several boys, all muddy after a football game perhaps, then the word *boys* is plural, more than one. Whatever, write down the 'owner' — either one *boy*, or many *boys*. Thus:

Boy (singular)
Boys (plural)

Now add to each, the apostrophe; which will give:

Boy'
Boys'

Now if it sounds right to do so, add an *s.*

The boy's legs (One boy) Sounds fine; so leave it.

The boys's legs (Two or more boys) Sounds awful, *boy-ses.*
So scrap the second *s.*

Sometimes, though, that second *s* does sound well enough; as in *John Keats's poetry* and *Henry James's stories.* Then you may add it.

If the above sounds too hassling, take comfort from the fact that these days fewer folk are bothering about the apostrophe of possession, and that its use will likely wither away. If you can recognise possession, though, and just stick an apostrophe before the *s*, you'll be 'correct' more often than not. And even when you're not, most readers will either not know, or at least not be confident enough to come out into the open and say so!

As was earlier indicated, there are a number of systems of grammar, and any of these will enlighten you in some way about the workings of our miracle language. Only traditional grammar, however, is prescriptive; that is, asserts that there is correct, and incorrect. The other grammars are descriptive, simply showing what is going on with those words and sentences we are using. Most people, when they speak of grammar, mean traditional grammar — nouns and prepositions, the objective case and subordinate clauses, past participles and pluperfect tense.

There are many traditional grammar and usage books around, and these are the ones mostly drawn on for Guides to writing and Courses on writing. Here are some of the so-called rules you'll find in such 'authorities'.

Every sentence should contain a verb

A verb is a *doing* (or *being*) word, and in general, every sentence does need at least one.

> Melanie down the road.

Melanie *what* down the road? *Ran? Called? Stared? Skidded?* Some verb is needed to relate *Melanie* to *down the road.*

> He that the hill was too high.

Thought? Judged? Had realised? Might have decided? Will tell?

> Every sentence a verb.

Should have? Shouldn't have? Will have? Demands?

Not every sentence though. Indeed, that sentence itself — *Not every sentence though* — doesn't have any verb! What it does have, traditional grammar would assert, is a verb understood. That is, understood by the reader to be there, although actually it's not. Thus:

> Not every sentence *(has)* though.

The situation this rule seems to be addressing is the sentence which has one verb and which the writer then divides into two, leaving one of the parts verbless.

> Bekky went through the park to the shops. Then over the bridge to Wendy's pad.

The alleged offence here is that the second sentence has no verb — *went* occurring only in the first sentence. The proposed remedies for this include use of conjunctions like *and, or* and *but*.

> Bekky went through the park to the shop and then over the bridge to Wendy's pad.

Commas can help to:

> Becky went through the park to the shop, then over the bridge to Wendy's pad.

While every major writer would one time or another have used verbless sentences, it is probably wisest to avoid them.

Who and Whom

Who and *whom* still get attention from traditionalists.

> The lass *who* gave me the book.

> The boy *to whom* I gave the book.

That is, *the person doing*, in this case the girl, gets *who*; and *the person done to*, the boy, gets *whom*.

The reasons for such a distinction go right back to highly inflected (word endings) languages, like Latin and Old English. (The *es* in *cyninges* is an inflected ending.) But *The boy who I gave the book to* ... is clear enough in meaning; so *whom* seems another usage on its way out.

Split Infinitive

Then there's the split infinitive. Elderly gentlemen with mulberry complexions write spluttering letters to the (better) newspapers about this enormity.

An infinitive is the general, unapplied form of a verb, as ... *to go*. When *to go* gets specific, applied use, it becomes *going*, or *gone*, or *will go*, or *has gone*, or *will have gone*, or *should be going*, or *went*. All verbs have this infinitive, basic form — *to eat, to cook, to think, to join, to hasten, to write, to translate;* even *to split*.

You split an infinitive when you place some word(s) between the *to* and the *stem word* of that infinitive: to *quietly* go, to *quickly* read, to *definitely* request.

According to the traditionalists, these should be: to go quietly, to read quickly, to request definitely. OR quietly to go, quickly to read, definitely to request.

This hostility towards the split infinitive is strange because there can be no rule from Latin about it. Latin infinitives are one-worders — *laudare*, to praise; *videre*, to see; *monere*, to advise, *audire*, to hear — so there's nothing to split anyway. The reasoning perhaps is that if you can't split a Latin infinitive, you shouldn't be allowed to split an English one. Well, ho hum?

When a correspondent to the London CHRONICLE berated George Bernard Shaw for writing *to suddenly go*, that irascible language 'reformer' responded, "Sir! Put this man out ... without interfering with his perfect freedom to suddenly go, to go suddenly or suddenly to go!" And the Canadian humorist Stephen Leacock wrote of the split infinitive: "We might even be willing to *sometimes so completely, in order to gain a particular effect,* split the infinitive ..." This sentence nicely interposes ten words between the two parts of the infinitive *to split!*

In North America, many Composition classes at tertiary institutions still outlaw the split infinitive.

Double Negative

Then there's the double negative:

I never ate no dinner.

This is intended to mean that no dinner has been eaten; that is, still hungry! The two negatives, *never* and *no,* act as intensifiers; simply increasing *no* to *NO!* Traditionalists maintain, however, that two such negatives cancel each other out. If you didn't eat *no* dinner, then you did eat *some* dinner; so you've no right to be hungry at all!

Double negatives have always been common as intensifiers. Chaucer used them, indeed, even triple negatives! *I nyl nat do no labour* = something like "I willn't not do no work!" — hardly a sentiment likely to be welcome these days at any Commonwealth Employment Office! But again, best to avoid double negs. As Holden Caulfield would put it, they get you a bad name!

Ending with a Preposition

I doubt that even those of the sager sort take very seriously these days: *Never end a sentence with a preposition.* Again, it's a Latin based injunction.

Prepositions are words like *by, with, from, to* and *for.* Here's *the station we leave from* should be, according to this rule, *Here's the station from which we leave.* Similarly, then: *this is the lock the key's for...* should perhaps be something like: *this is the lock for which this is the key.*

Winston Churchill summed this one up. (Oops! Summed up this one.)

This is the sort of English up with which I shall not put.

Certain words, by the way, customarily take particular prepositions, as different *from.* Different *to* is also much used nowadays, though frowned on by the more strict. Different *than* is thought about as ignorant as you can get, short perhaps of *Ta very much!*

Floating Phrases and Participles

Then there are floating phrases and participles. If you separate a phrase from the word or whatever it goes with, you invite confusions.

Cassandra ran down the street with no children.

I met a man coming from a farm with seven horses.

Is it Cassandra or the street that has *no children?* Is it the man, or the farm, that has the *seven horses?*

Participles are parts of verbs, like *going, given, stated, gone,* as in *was going, had been given, is stated* and *should be gone.* As with phrases, confusions can arise if these get separated from whatever they are supposed to be linked with.

Dexter waited happily on the station. Singing most of the time, the trains came and went.

Here, it sounds as if it's the trains that are singing most of the time! *Singing* really goes with *Dexter;* and the sentence could easily be recast to make this clear.

> Dexter waited happily on the station. He sang most of the time, as the trains came and went.

Or if you want to keep the participle *singing*:

> Dexter, singing most of the time as the trains came and went, waited happily on the station.

Punctuation

Finally, in this pod of formal elements, is punctuation.

Even the traditionalists have all but given up on absolutes here. You punctuate to make sense — that is, to break up into units of meaning; to indicate pause and stop; to generate rhythm; to emphasise and draw attention to; to distinguish a statement from a question; to indicate who's speaking — purposes like these. Reading aloud can help give a sense of how punctuation is working.

> "Brett," said Tony, "is dead."
> Brett said Tony is dead.

The punctuation here is a matter of life and death to Brett and Tony! And of course, from one's childhood, the marvel of:

> King Charles walked and talked half an hour after his head was cut off.

is rendered entirely unremarkable by a little punctuation:

> King Charles walked and talked. Half an hour after, his head was cut off.

As with grammar, it is probably more effective to absorb punctuating skills from well written passages, than to adopt rules from some established authority.

The sentence is the basic unit. It begins with a capital letter and ends mostly with a full stop; though it can also end with a question mark, exclamation mark, a dash, or even a row of dots ... Many sentences have only the one main statement. Others have two or more main statements, or one main statement and one or several supporting (subordinate) statements.

> As soon as Andrea reached the supermarket, she found it had closed.

The main statement is *she found it had closed.* The other statement, *As soon as Andrea reached the supermarket,* tells only the 'when' of the main statement.

Two or more main statements can be joined by words like *and* or *but,* or indeed by some form of punctuation like a semi-colon.

Andrea reached the supermarket and found it closed.
You can stay here or you can come with me.

Andrea reached the supermarket; she found it closed.
You can stay here; or you can come with me.

Note the use of two commas in the sentence below.

On the fifth day, HOWEVER, the rain cleared.

Many would write this as:

HOWEVER, on the fifth day the rain cleared.

This seems acceptable nowadays, though to begin a sentence with *However* was once regarded as unacceptable.

Commas direct sense, or meaning, and they can also give emphasis.

He said with great gusto that he was ready to eat.
He said, with great gusto, that he was ready to eat.

Commas in the latter seem to draw attention to the *great gusto* and so foreground it.

Semi-colons might be thought of as red lights that stay on longer than comma red lights. They also divide statements or sentences where the two parts are more evenly balanced in importance — that is, less the big strong main segment and the little deferential supporting segment.

Dinner would be late; the stove was out of order.

If you'd written this: *Dinner would be late because the stove was out of order,* that second segment (clause) *because the stove was out of order* would be a subordinate one. It simply gives an explanation for the main clause, *Dinner would be late.* With the semi-colon, you get the sentence to being nearer perhaps to two main statements?

Few writers use the colon very effectively, as it doesn't have a particularly well-defined function. You could probably say that it is used when the red light flashes a full stop but for some reason you don't want a final break and a new sentence; you want to hold it all together as one complete sentence. So:

> For some reason you don't want a full stop: you want to
> hold it all together as one complete sentence.

As will be apparent, you could use comma, semi-colon, colon or indeed full stop after *full stop* above. It's largely a matter of how you want it read.

You know, don't you, how to show question and exclamation?

You certainly should!

Capital letters go to proper nouns; and if you want to know what proper nouns are, they are names which take capital letters! The obvious ones are the names of individual people, nations, cities, institutions, titles ... as Robertson, New Zealand, Christchurch, the Catholic Cathedral and the Commonwealth Bank, Prince Charles and God. Others, you would find listed in those books on usage. There are a few uncertain, as particular centuries. Mostly it's nineteenth century; but some prefer Nineteenth Century.

This leaves direct speech. The mechanics of this will probably be clear to you from your reading and from Chapter 6 on Dialogue. Mostly, and most safely, it's inverted commas, single or double; though the dash has been used, as have italics.

Inverted commas have quite definite rules of precedence in relation to other items of punctuation. Note in these examples which goes where:

> "Hi!" he said.

> "Will you indeed?" She picked up ...

> "I'm going up the hill," he told her, "but when I get back I'll
> expect the tea made. OK?"

Here are two passages from Katherine Mansfield. The first is from "The Wind Blows", the second from "Bliss". Check out each instance of punctuation carefully, for purpose and effect. You might ask yourself, too, why in the first passage there is no question mark after *And why have you got that mane of hair on your forehead*; nor any exclamation mark following *Go to hell*.

There seems no obvious answer; the sentences are such straightforward question and exclamation.

> " For heaven's sake keep the front door shut! Go round to the back," shouts someone. And then she hears Bogey:

> "Mother, you're wanted on the telephone. Telephone, Mother. It's the butcher."

> How hideous life is — revolting, simply revolting. ... And now her hat-elastic's snapped. Of course it would. She'll wear her old tam and slip out the back way. But Mother has seen.

> "Matilda. Matilda. Come back im-me-diately! What on earth have you got on your head? It looks like a tea cosy. And why have you got that mane of hair on your forehead."

> "I can't come back, Mother. I'll be late for my lesson."

> "Come back immediately!"

> She won't. She won't. She hates Mother. "Go to hell," she shouts, running down the road.

> ....

> "My dear," said Mrs Norman Knight, "you know our shame. We are victims of time and train. We live in Hampshire. It has been so nice."

> "I'll come into the hall with you" said Bertha. "I loved having you. But you must not miss the last train. That's so awful, isn't it?"

> "Have a whisky, Knight, before you go?" called Harry.

> "No thanks, old chap."

> Bertha squeezed her hand for that as she shook it.

> "Good night, good-bye," she cried from the top step, feeling that this self of hers was taking leave of them forever.

Changing Language

Finally, language change; which is continual, with social evolution demanding additional vocabularies, (Old English hardly required a term for *motorway!*) and writers, especially poets, pressing the customary beyond its seeming limits. (Old English poets loved creating evocative terms for the most common words, as *wavesteed* for *ship*, and some fifty such for *ocean*, like *whale road, fish home* and *seal bath*.)

To make new words, we still dip back to Latin or classical Greek — *television* and *patriarchal* and *feminist and helicopter*. Occasionally we even borrow the same word twice, at different times or from different directions — as *church* and *shirt* and *shrub* from Old English and *kirk* and *skirt* and *scrub* from Scandinavian; and *guarantee* (North French) with *warranty* (Central French). We also yoke old words together to make new ones, as the Old English so often did with, for example, their *mod*, which meant *mind, spirit, mood*; so creating *modcreaft* (*intelligence)* and *gleadmodnes* (*kindness)* and, indeed, some hundred other *mod*-something! Hence our present day compounding as with *gentleman* and *housekeeper* and *doomsday*. Often, too, we take borrowed words and add OE suffixes — the French *gentle* + OE *ness* = *gentleness*.

All this has given us what is perhaps the richest language in the world — at half a million words, probably larger than any other; with an enormous range of subtle meanings and tones — near, but not quite, synonyms. For example, from sources Old English, French and Latin:

Rise	mount	ascend
Ask	question	interrogate
Goodness	virtue	probity
Holy	sacred	consecrated
Fire	flame	conflagration

We even have words that were translated from Latin into Old English then 'modernised' over the course of time — *spiritus sanctus* to *halig gast* to *holy ghost!*

Likewise, writers produced extraordinary and evocative new uses for old words. The poet Marvell's — *A green thought in a green shade* — both uses of *green* are, to say the least, unusual? Shakespeare's *Dark backward and abysm of time* and (the advent of twilight) are unusual, too.

Light thickens. In a way, the expressions don't make sense, yet they startle, arrest and resonate. A twentieth century example would be e e cummings' Cambridge ladies who live in *furnished souls*. (This eccentric American poet eschews the use of capital letters and establishes a great deal of his own unique grammar and word usage too!)

Sadly, not all word changes act to enrich our vocabulary. Some impoverish it by exterminating good words or adding jargon and trendy words. An example of the former is *partial*, which used to mean *inclined to favour;* but this has been overwhelmed by *in part.* There seems no other word with quite the *inclined to favour* meaning — *bias* being harsher and perhaps more *inclined not to favour? Disinterested* looks like being another loss. It should mean roughly the opposite of *biased* and (the old) *partial* — that is, *no personal axe to grind, no personal stake in.* Hence *a disinterested observer,* whose report can therefore be confidently credited. The word, though, is rapidly becoming just a synonym for *uninterested.*

As for *jargon,* this tends to pervert language by rendering meaning obscure rather than opening it up, and often by giving some mystical, priestly status to an area of special or cult-like interest. Computer-speak seems to have produced some jargon, for instance; though there have been some innovative and lively new uses of language from there too; and of course, many technical and academic terms are simply unavoidable. They are employed to distinguish specialised meanings in particular fields.

In *literary criticism,* for example, *criticism* does not mean *being critical of,* or *trashing,* but rather *evaluating, assessing.* A book of literary criticism would likely praise some of the poetry it discusses and pan (or in the popular sense, criticise) some of it. Likewise, in such literary criticism the term *tragedy* has a meaning differing from *tragedy* in a Sunday newspaper. The first is a literary genre, a particular kind of play or novel with its origins in classical Greece. The second, the popular sense, means *calamity, disaster.* Writers, perhaps more than any other group, should be concerned to preserve and defend the precision and expressiveness and wondrous vitality of our precious language.

Horace, the urbane Roman poet who still managed to sink a few javelins into the decadent values of his time, once noted: *Saepe stilum verte, bonum librum scripturus.* The first three words mean *Often invert the pen* (that is, use the eraser on the other end — rub out). So, loosely translated — *If you want good writing, edit frequently.* Which is about as effective a summary of this chapter as you could get in six words?

11

Where To From Here?

F iction, we remarked earlier, is a tale told; and quality fiction represents the top-of-the range among such tales.

The reason WUTHERING HEIGHTS still resonates across a century and a half; that THE CATCHER IN THE RYE grabbed and shook a whole generation; that BLISS continues to snipe so tellingly at metropolitan complacencies; is that each author was able to match a vision of what underlies the-way-things-are, with the *writing skills* to convey this vision compellingly. Most of us would not expect to win quite such laurels (though who knows?); but what we can do, is steadily upgrade our own professional skills and so close the gap somewhat. Which is pretty much what this GUIDE sets out to help you do.

As for the way of life you as a writer are committing yourself to, it is equally open-ended. Within the limits of your talent, you'll find numberless opportunities to tell tales about people getting on with their lives; confronting challenges and celebrating achievement and reeling from loss. Even if you make little money from your writing and your fame burns so, so dimly, you'll hardly find a more satisfying nor a more FUN way to fill a life than in the role of Makaris, of Bard, of the magical spinner of words. Because there will always be folk wondering, as the love poet Catullus did way back in Roman times, *Cui hunc novum librum dabo?* "Who will I give this book to?"

Appendix

Titles Referred to in
WRITING QUALITY FICTION

ADAM BEDE, George Eliot.

A FRINGE OF LEAVES, Patrick White.

AFTER THE FIRST DEATH, Robert Cormier.

A MIDSUMMER NIGHT'S DREAM, William Shakespeare.

ANTONY AND CLEOPATRA, William Shakespeare.

A PASSAGE TO INDIA, E. M. Forster.

A PERFECT BEAST, Kay Gregory.

AS YOU LIKE IT, William Shakespeare.

AUTUMN, Terence Crawford.

BILLY BATCHELOR, Shirley McLaughlin.

BLEAK HOUSE, Charles Dickens.

BLISS, Katherine Mansfield.

BRING LARKS AND HEROES, Thomas Keneally.

CABIN FEVER, Elizabeth Jolley.

CHARADES, Janette Turner Hospital.

DAS KAPITAL, Karl Marx.

DR JEKYLL AND MR HYDE, R. L. Stevenson.

EARLY VICTORIAN NOVELISTS, David Cecil.

EMMA, Jane Austen.

GREAT EXPECTATIONS, Charles Dickens.

HAMLET, William Shakespeare.

HENRY IV PT I, William Shakespeare.

HERSELF SURPRISED, Joyce Cary.

HUCKLEBERRY FINN, Mark Twain.

HUMPHREY CLINKER, Tobias Smollett.

I CAN JUMP PUDDLES, Alan Marshall.

IT, William Mayne.

JANE EYRE, Charlotte Bronte.

JOHNNO, David Malouf.

JOSEPH ANDREWS, Henry Fielding.

JULIUS CAESAR, William Shakespeare.

KING LEAR, William Shakespeare.

LIFE: A USER'S MANUAL, Georges Perec.

LUCINDA BRAYFORD, Martin Boyd.

MACBETH, William Shakespeare.

MANSFIELD PARK, Jane Austen.

MEASURE FOR MEASURE, William Shakespeare.

MISS PEABODY'S INHERITANCE, Elizabeth Jolley.

MODERN LOVE, George Meredith.

MRS DALLOWAY, Virginia Woolf.

NORTHANGER ABBEY, Jane Austen.

ONCE WERE WARRIORS, Alan Duff.

OTHELLO, William Shakespeare.

PEREGRINE PICKLE, Tobias Smollett.

PERSUASION, Jane Austen.

PRIDE AND PREJUDICE, Jane Austen.

PUDD'NHEAD WILSON, Mark Twain.

ROBINSON CRUSOE, Daniel Defoe.

RODERICK RANDOM, Tobias Smollett.

ROMEO AND JULIET, William Shakespeare.

SHIRLEY, Charlotte Bronte.

SMALL WORLD, David Lodge.

STATUES AGAINST THE SKY, Ken Moon.

STILL LIFE, A. S. Byatt.

TESS OF THE D'URBERVILLES, Thomas Hardy.

THE AENEID, Virgil.

THE ART OF FICTION, David Lodge.

"The Ballad of the Drover", Henry Lawson.

THE BAY OF NOON, Shirley Hazzard.

THE CATCHER IN THE RYE, J. D. Salinger.

THE CANTERBURY TALES, Geoffrey Chaucer.

THE CHILDREN'S BACH, Helen Garner.

THE COLOR PURPLE, Alice Walker.

THE ENGLISH NOVEL: FORM AND FUNCTION, Dorothy Van
Ghent.

THE ENVOY FROM MIRROR CITY, Janet Frame.

THE FRENCH LIEUTENANT'S WOMAN, John Fowles.

THE GOOD SOLDIER, Ford Maddox Ford.

THE JERSEY SHORE, William Mayne.

THE LIFE AND OPINIONS OF TRISTRAM SHANDY, Laurence
Sterne.

THE MASTER OF THE GROVE, Victor Kelleher.

THE MERCHANT OF VENICE, William Shakespeare.

THE MILL ON THE FLOSS, George Eliot.

THE ORCHARD, Drusilla Modjeska.

THE PENGUIN DICTIONARY OF LITERARY TERMS.

THE PICTURE OF DORIAN GRAY, Oscar Wilde.

THE REHEARSAL, George Villiers.

THE RETURN OF THE NATIVE, Thomas Hardy.

THE SEAGULL, Anton Chekov.

THE SHIPPING NEWS, Annie Proulx.

THE THEBAN PLAYS, Sophocles.

THE TRANSIT OF VENUS, Shirley Hazzard.

THE VIRGIN IN THE GARDEN, A.S. Byatt.

THE WAVES, Virginia Woolf.

"The Wind Blows," Katherine Mansfield.

THE WRITING BOOK, Kate Grenville.

THE YEARS, Virginia Woolf.

THREE MEN IN A BOAT, Jerome K. Jerome.

TIRRA LIRRA BY THE RIVER, Jessica Anderson.

TOM FOBBLE'S DAY, Alan Garner.

TOM JONES, Henry Fielding.

TOM SAWYER, Mark Twain.

TROILUS AND CRESSIDA, William Shakespeare.

TWELFTH NIGHT, William Shakespeare.

ULTRAMARINE, Malcolm Lowry.

ULYSSES, Homer.

WAITING FOR GODOT, Samuel Beckett.

WHO'S AFRAID OF VIRGINIA WOOLF? Edward Albee.

WRITE YOUR LIFE: A GUIDE TO AUTOBIOGRAPHY, Ken Moon.

WUTHERING HEIGHTS, Emily Bronte.

WYCLIFFE AND THE DUNES MYSTERY, W.J. Burley.

ZEN AND THE ART OF MOTOR CYCLE MAINTENANCE, Robert
  Pirsig.

Index